LOST VICTORIAN BRITAIN

GAVIN STAMP is an architectural historian and writer, who for many years was Chairman of the Twentieth-Century Society. His other books include *Britain's Lost Cities* and *Edwin Lutyens Houses* (both published by Aurum), *The Memorial to the Missing of the Somme* and *The Changing Metropolis: Earliest Photographs of London 1839-1879*.

Praise for Gavin Stamp's *Britain's Lost Cities*:

'This masterful book should be placed in every council planning committee in the country'
Tristram Hunt, *BBC History Magazine*

'An engrossing, no-punches-pulled denunciation of the wilful destruction of our urban landscapes since the 1950s'
The Times

'Nineteen elegant, well-informed, rueful, sometimes bitter essays... accompanied by a gallery of intensely evocative, occasionally stunning photographs of what we have lost'
David Kynaston, *Times Literary Supplement*

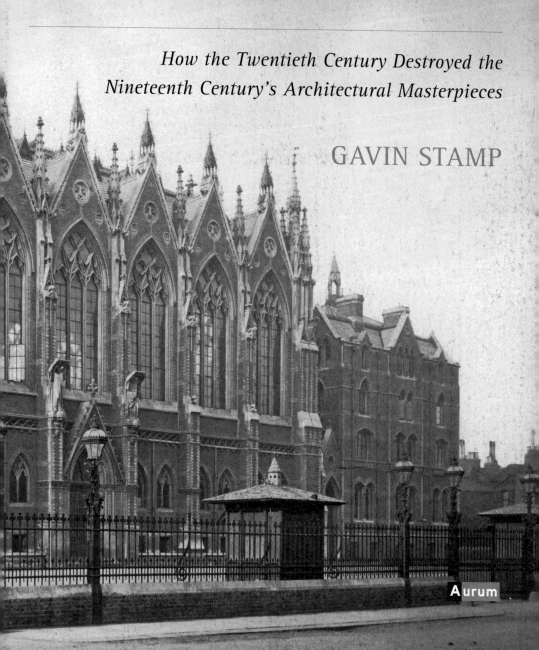

LOST VICTORIAN BRITAIN

*How the Twentieth Century Destroyed the
Nineteenth Century's Architectural Masterpieces*

GAVIN STAMP

Aurum

Dedicated to The Victorian Society

First published in Great Britain
2010 by Aurum Press Ltd
74–77 White Lion Street, London N1 9PF
www.aurumpress.co.uk

This paperback edition first published in 2013 by Aurum Press Ltd

A catalogue record for this book is available from the British Library.
ISBN 978 1 78131 018 2

10 9 8 7 6 5 4 3 2 1
2017 2016 2015 2014 2013
Designed by Peter Ward
Printed in China

◀◀ The great hall of the Columbia Market in Bethnal Green photographed by Horatio Nelson King in 1872.

CONTENTS

The Caledonia Road Church, the first great Presbyterian temple in Glasgow by Alexander 'Greek' Thomson, gutted by arson in 1965 and then partially demolished; photograph by Thomas Annan, c.1860

INTRODUCTION

How could one not love St Pancras Station? An extraordinary and huge red-brick and stone Gothic Revival hotel with a riotous skyline of spires and pinnacles attached to a stupendous single-span iron-and-glass train shed: the whole complex rich, solid, romantic (especially if you have seen a reproduction of John O'Connor's evocative 1884 painting of St Pancras from the West at sunset), intriguing, and altogether thrilling . . . And yet it is not that long since this great London landmark, something so exciting while working perfectly well as a railway station, was threatened with annihilation as national politicians and the mediocrities who were busy running down British Railways disparaged it as ugly, ridiculous and out of date.

In 1966, as a schoolboy, I joined the Victorian Society to support the campaign to save St Pancras (and King's Cross next door). Soon after, the 'Vic Soc' organised a visit to St Pancras Chambers and I went along, and so was able to see Gilbert Scott's amazing grand staircase under its Gothic vault, dowdy but intact, as well as to hear the architect Roderick Gradidge explain how modern services could easily be introduced into the massive, run-down building to turn it back into an hotel.

I was fascinated by Victorian London. Inspired by the writings of Nikolaus Pevsner, John Betjeman and Ian Nairn, I explored the excitingly diverse and often eccentric legacy of the 19th century in the capital. It was unfashionable, but that no more deterred me than did the grime and neglect which so many regarded as sufficient reason to demolish or modernise. In fact, I found that the effects of time and weather added to the sublime glamour of Victorian architecture. But I was also already well aware that it had its enemies. One day, at school, workmen arrived to hack off part of the moulded stiff-leaf column capitals in the open 'cloisters' between the big, red-brick and terra-cotta mid Victorian buildings (Charles Barry junior: 1866–70) in south London that I had grown to love, so cheap, crude glazing could be installed by a wretched modern architect. I, and several of my contemporaries, were dismayed at such gratuitous vandalism: why couldn't this proposed improvement be carried out with sensitivity and respect?

Much of my education consisted of discovering the past only to find that it was under threat, disregarded, disparaged. Near my school, solid, colourful Victorian villas were being pulled down

▲ The ruins of the Crystal Palace: panoramic photograph by T.H. Everitt & Son taken the morning after the fire on 30th November 1936.

for redevelopment, while further up the hill, the forlorn, haunting site of the Crystal Palace spoke of lost Victorian glories. At the end of my first year at university, in the summer of that year of revolution, 1968, I decided to go north – by train, of course – to explore the great Victorian industrial cities that, as a southern suburban Englishman, I had never really been told about, let alone taken to. Leeds, Manchester, Liverpool, Newcastle . . . here were smoke-blackened but immensely rewarding places, so different from what I had been used to, full of splendid Victorian buildings, but then being systematically trashed, bulldozed, redeveloped in a frenzy of naïve utopianism combined with self-hatred in favour of . . . what? I did not care, being somehow immune to or blinkered to the appeal of the Modern Movement vision.

Intrigued by the history of the heroic Midland Railway that had built St Pancras, I took its route even further north, travelling on its magnificently engineered main-line over the Pennines, the Settle and Carlisle, which I had learned was threatened, needless to say, with closure. Once upon a time, the Midland's Pullman expresses had run between those most obscure of saints –

St Pancras to St Enoch – but in Glasgow the trains now ended up in Central Station. On my second visit to the city, in 1973, I actually stayed at the St Enoch Hotel. The great train shed behind it was empty of trains and just used as a car park, but the hotel itself had recently been redecorated in a sympathetic neo-Victorian manner by British Transport Hotels. The building was grand, comfortable and splendid. How dismaying therefore – but how very typical of Glasgow, as I would later discover – to learn that within four years both had been destroyed: the solid, serviceable hotel demolished; the great train shed – which could, with a little thought and intelligence, have been made into a conference centre, like its Midland cousin in Manchester – removed, to be replaced, a while later, by a tawdry glass shopping centre.

Four decades on, the surviving architectural legacy of the Victorians looks very different. The vigorous civic pride that lay behind all those soot-black town halls, both Gothic and Classic, now seems healthy and admirable. Politicians, in their entrenched ignorance and philistinism, are still encouraging the replacement of sound and serviceable school buildings, but most Victorian

and Edwardian public buildings have now been cleaned and repaired while ordinary 19th-century houses are generally far more popular than their 20th-century replacements. The Victorians no longer seem so absurd; a modern biography of the great ecclesiastical designer Augustus Pugin has won prizes, enjoyed critical acclaim and reached a wide audience. The best Victorian churches now seem not only expressive of their time but creative works of art as valuable, and as representative, as the cathedrals of the Middle Ages.

By her actions rather than words, Mrs Thatcher may have tarnished the 'Victorian values' she espoused, but the merits of the best Victorian buildings now seem self-evident. Not only are they colourful, enjoyable and life-enhancing, but they are well and solidly built, practical, serviceable and, so often, perfectly adaptable to modern needs. With increasing consciousness of the need for sustainability and of how much 'embodied energy' there is in our old building stock, it becomes irresponsible to destroy them unless absolutely necessary. In contrast, so many of the replacement new buildings of the 1960s have proved so inadequate that they themselves have since been replaced. So

much of that destruction I witnessed back in 1968 now seems an unnecessary tragedy.

The change in attitudes is best exemplified by the happy fate of St Pancras. Threatened with demolition in 1966 and neglected for years afterwards, the station has re-emerged into public consciousness as a splendid gateway to Europe. The re-vamped station is a now triumphant success: past and future can co-exist. Eurostar trains now run into William Barlow's great train shed, so well and imaginatively adapted, while Gilbert Scott's Midland Grand Hotel is also being brought back to life. All this has been possible partly because the Victorians built to last. Thanks to their ambition and vision, it no longer seems hopelessly impractical to think of making a 19th-century railway terminus into an inter-continental interchange for the 21st century. Back in 1966, that was evident to Pevsner, to Betjeman, to Wayland Kennet, to the Victorian Society and, for that matter, to me; but why couldn't most people see through the dirt and grime to the potential of that great building almost half a century ago? The answer is simple: myopia and prejudice.

'Whatever may be said in favour of the Victorians, it is pretty generally admitted that few of them were to be trusted within reach of a trowel and a pile of bricks'. So wrote P.G. Wodehouse in 1937 of his fictional Walsingford Hall, a 'celebrated eyesore in all its startling revolting hideousness' built of glazed red brick midway through the reign of Queen Victoria.[1] This was typical of contemporary attitudes towards most of the architecture erected in Britain during that era.

'Victorian' has often been used as a pejorative term, although the strict dictionary definition of the adjective is, 'of or relating to the reign of Queen Victoria (1837–1901)'. 'Forty years ago,' recalled the historian of fashion and taste, James Laver, in 1966, 'the word "Victorian" was simply a term of abuse; it stood for all that was stuffy, heavy, and overladen with ornament'.[2] Although there has been, for half a century and more, a serious historical reappraisal of the achievements of the Victorians and we are conscious today of our continuing debt to them, the prejudice still lingers. It has been particularly strong – and destructive – when applied to their architecture. In consequence, far too many imaginatively designed, visually stimulating, soundly constructed and sumptuously decorated buildings – often conspicuous monuments of their time which have defined many of our cities – have been needlessly and stupidly demolished. These Victorian victims – sometimes of accident or war but mostly ignorance and prejudice – are the theme of this book.

For much of the 20th century, Victorian architecture was conventionally held to be self-evidently hideous and ridiculous, not to be taken seriously. The future Lord Clark of Civilization recalled how in Oxford in 1927, when he was writing his pioneering study of the Gothic Revival:

> it was universally believed that Ruskin had built Keble, and that it was the ugliest building in the world. Undergraduates and young dons used to break off on their afternoon walks in order to have a good laugh at the quadrangle.[3]

Nothing much had changed by 1950, at least in Cambridge, when Nikolaus Pevsner gave his inaugural Slade Lecture on the subject of the Victorian architect and designer Matthew Digby Wyatt and 'the undergraduates found it a huge joke and laughed so much that I had to step off the platform and say: "This is not funny."'[4] And the condescending smirks continued among many who ought to have known better. Two decades later, Pevsner could still complain,

> The public at large is only just getting over its giggles where Victorian building is concerned. Few still are ready to look with open eyes and open minds, and even the experts who spend their time among buildings of power and elegance have only rarely accepted the duty of seeing and evaluating what is comparatively so near to them in time.[5]

No wonder, therefore, that many Victorian buildings were mutilated in the cause of superior taste when they could not be swept away, their richly textured polychromatic interiors toned down, if possible, with paint or whitewash. Taste, after all, is always confident in its rightness, blissfully unaware of its ephemerality and fickleness. For much of the 20th century only the creations of the great Victorian engineers, triumphant in scale and practicality, could be admired while contemporary productions of the architects were dismissed, particularly by their modern counterparts. 'The word "Victorian" was derogatory in the 1920s and '30s,' John Betjeman recalled, some three decades later.

> Victorian was associated in the minds of architects who had been brought up in the arts and crafts tradition of the 1900s with hard and unsympathetic imitation of gothic and vulgar things like conservatories, stations and hotels which were not considered within the realms of art at all.[6]

Of course, every generation despises the taste of its predecessor, so that, as the English architect and writer H.S. Goodhart-Rendel put it to members of the newborn Victorian Society in 1958: 'Real beauties are obscured to us by the eternal predisposition of each generation to dislike what father liked so much'.[7] So the 1970s reacted against the bland mechanical austerity of modernism, just as the Victorians were repelled by the 'hole in the wall' domestic architecture of the Georgians exemplified by Gower Street. But the rejection of the Victorians by the post-Victorians would seem to have been of a greater intensity. Exacerbated by the intervention of the Great War, an enormous gulf opened up between the Late Victorians and Edwardians and their children, the generation that reached maturity between the world wars. To them – as is confirmed by so many autobiographies – their parents were grotesque caricatures of stuffiness and hypocrisy, for whom there was scant sympathy. The whole Victorian Age came to be seen as dark and oppressive, at once sinister and ludicrous, and there was a violent reaction against its legacy in favour of a clean, uncluttered modernity. And the buildings left behind by the Victorians, so prominent, so solid, so confident, so extraordinary, became the targets of particularly virulent abuse.

The attitudes of the Bloomsbury Group epitomised this anti-Victorian feeling; Lytton Strachey damned the Albert Memorial with clever sarcasm and Virginia Woolf could imagine someone never having seen anything 'at once so indecent, so hideous, so monumental' as that belated expression of Victorian taste, the Victoria Memorial.[8] Even more extreme views were elicited by more distant buildings in what can now be appreciated as a most remarkable Gothic Revival city: the travel writer Robert Byron, after visiting 'that architectural Sodom, Bombay' in 1930, wrote that, 'The nineteenth century devised nothing lower than the municipal buildings of British India. Their ugliness is positive, demonic'.[9]

As Kenneth Clark had discovered, it was the ostensibly educated who led the way in dismissing 'hideous' Victorian architecture (popular taste perhaps lagged behind and took longer to feel uncomfortable with ornament and sumptuousness). This prejudice was conventionally expressed by a Cambridge don, the historian G.M. Trevelyan, when, evidently unaware of the blinkers imposed by his own time, he wrote in his *English Social History* that,

The most refined and educated classes were as bad as any: the monstrosities of architecture erected by order of the Dons of Oxford and Cambridge Colleges in the days of William Butterfield and Alfred Waterhouse give daily pain to posterity.[10]

The curious thing about such myopic dismissals is that while their authors could be profoundly interested in 19th-century politics and social history, and were able to enjoy the contemporary literature and might even be prepared to consider Victorian music and painting, architecture remained beyond the pale. Trevelyan, despite his blinkers, could claim in 1949 that, 'The period of reaction against the nineteenth century is over; the era of dispassionate historical valuation has begun'.[11] Yet, as Pevsner, the second chairman of the Victorian Society, complained in 1963:

As far as the knowledge and appreciation of architecture goes, the Victorian age is the most neglected of all ages. The situation is strikingly contrary to that in literature, music and painting – perhaps for good reasons. [. . .] For the time being the fact remains that the layman, including most architects and most architectural historians, just has not got the information available to pass any worth-while judgements on Victorian architecture.[12]

This was not, in fact, altogether true as there had been a precious few in the field – architects and writers – who, for the preceding four decades, had endeavoured to look at Victorian buildings with an unprejudiced eye and encouraged others to try and understand them.

The pioneer in this was the architect and historian, Harry Stuart Goodhart-Rendel – 'the father of us all,' as Kenneth Clark described him. Having begun to practise in the Edwardian period and having known many older, Late-Victorian architects, Goodhart-Rendel seemed to have had a direct line to the High Victorians like William Butterfield, the idiosyncratic architect of Keble College. As early as 1919 he was writing (in the *Architectural Review*) about the Victorian churches of Brighton. For the following three decades Goodhart-Rendel gave lectures about Victorian Architecture (among other things) but while these were popular, it must be feared that his audiences found them entertaining rather than enlightening. The prejudice remained, and it was assumed that the subject was intrinsically funny. And it was unfortunate that the lectures were only gathered together as a book, entitled *English Architecture Since the Regency*, as late as 1953.

Goodhart-Rendel lived just long enough to be a founder of the Victorian Society in 1958. In that year, John Betjeman noted, 'While all the rest of us were still looking at Georgian, he has for years been going ahead and looking at Victorian buildings, sifting the good from the bad and making notes about them for us which we have all copied and found invaluable'.[13] As a subtle, succinct interpreter of Victorian architecture he remains unequalled.

Kenneth Clark's study of the Gothic Revival, published in 1928, was a pioneering work of scholarship, but suffered from his confident assumption that the Revival 'produced so little on which our eyes can rest without pain'.[14]

Furthermore, its scope also ended at the very point at which Victorian Gothic was becoming interesting. As Clark confessed in the second (1949) edition: 'almost too late, I realized that the greatest architects of the movement were precisely those whom my contemporaries thought most insufferable, Street and Butterfield'.[15] Clark's book had no immediate successors, but in 1938 a thorough and well-informed survey of Victorian church architecture appeared. Entitled *Church Builders of the Nineteenth Century*, it was the work of the Revd Basil F.L. Clarke. Although the author later confessed that he 'did not altogether avoid the temptation to present the Victorians as comic. They were, of course – but so are all human beings . . .'[16] , the book is remarkable for taking the buildings seriously, but churches – for reasons pious rather than intellectual – were to some degree exempt from the general condemnation of Victorian buildings.

There were a few other publications to show that interest was stirring, though none was widely read. *Amphion, or, The Nineteenth Century* was a witty and stimulating survey published in 1930 by the Hull architect Dudley Harbron, who was sure that his subject had what was necessary in a good story, that is, to make the reader laugh or shudder. The book also took what became a conventional line, the quite erroneous notion that all that was wrong with Victorian architecture stemmed from the patronage of the rising middle class. Five years later came the posthumous publication of the lectures by the old Arts and Crafts architect, W.R. Lethaby, on his hero Philip Webb, who was almost the only Victorian to be universally praised in generally critical surveys of architecture – although that did not prevent many of his beautifully made houses from being mutilated or demolished (see below). It was also just about permissible to admire the work of Webb's prolific contemporary, Norman Shaw, and in 1940 a biography was published by Reginald Blomfield. This, too, was written by an elderly architect who had known his subject, but his aim was to rescue Shaw from oblivion and to

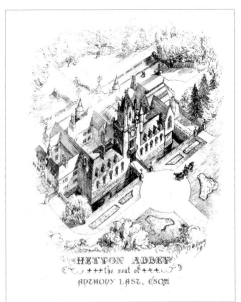

◀ 'Hetton Abbey': axonometric drawing by J.D.M. Harvey used as the frontispiece to Evelyn Waugh's novel, *A Handful of Dust*, 1934.

present him as a pioneer of revived Classicism, to whom 'more than anyone is due the recovery of architecture from the dull conventions of the Victorian era'.[17]

Meanwhile, a younger generation was beginning to find Victorian art amusing rather than simply awful. A 'Victorian Revival' can be dated from 1923 when two Oxford undergraduates, Robert Byron and Harold Acton, attempted to mount an exhibition about the taste of the 1840s until the enterprise was banned by the proctors. But not all Bright Young Things took an interest in the Victorians as an elaborate joke in order to feel superior to middle-class attitudes. Evelyn Waugh (1903–66) began to take Victorian art and architecture seriously and in 1934 he published a novel, *A Handful of Dust*, whose frontispiece was an axonometric view of a moated and turreted Gothic Revival country house drawn by the accomplished architectural perspectivist J.D.M. Harvey. This, Hetton Abbey, could also have been Wodehouse's Walsingford Hall except that Waugh did not mock its sentimental romantic Mediaevalisms. 'They were not in the fashion,' he had the house owner realise.

> Twenty years ago people had liked half timber and old pewter; now it was urns and colonnades; but the time would come . . . when opinion would reinstate Hetton in its proper place. Already it was referred to as 'amusing,' and a very civil young man had asked permission to photograph it for an architectural review.[18]

This last was surely a dig at Waugh's friend and contemporary, John Betjeman, who by now was actually working at the *Architectural Review* in London. Betjeman had begun by finding Victorian architecture funny, as is evident from his rather juvenile 1933 book, *Ghastly Good Taste*, in which he argues that 'chaos' resulted from the rise of the 'Middle Class, which represents industrialism' after the passing of the 1832 Reform Act. By the end of the decade, however, he was not only interested in Arts and Crafts architects, like Charles Voysey, who seemed to be pioneers of modernism but was well on the way to becoming a serious defender of unloved Victorian buildings and, as John Summerson later

put it, 'an illuminant and a sanction' through whom 'kindliness towards Victorian architecture is permitted to thousands whose habits of mind would drive them in a quite other direction'.[19]

Another Oxford contemporary and contributor to the 'Archie Rev' was the artist and writer Osbert Lancaster who, in 1938, published the first volume of his invaluable and influential cartoon history of architecture, *Pillar to Post*. In this, although he took the usual line that, 'While the more ambitious nineteenth-century manifestations of the Gothic spirit in architecture may, with very few exceptions, be dismissed as deplorable,' he drew such manifestations with affection as well as humour and earned the everlasting debt of historians by both illustrating and labelling such styles as '*Kensington Italianate*', '*Pont Street Dutch*' and the indispensable '*Edwardian Baroque*' (not to mention later ones like '*Aldwych Farcical*', '*Stockbrokers Tudor*' and '*Pseudish*').

During the Second World War, German bombs and rockets were not at all discriminating in the architectural quality of their targets and so made Victorian losses seem almost as tragic as those of

▲ 'Municipal Gothic' drawn by Osbert Lancaster for his book *Pillar to Post* published in 1938.

Georgian terraces or Wren churches. The wartime books on *The Bombed Buildings of Britain* by J.M. Richards and John Summerson included photographs of casualties designed by Pugin, Butterfield, Street and Pearson. Nikolaus Pevsner, as caretaker editor of the *Architectural Review*, published articles on Victorian themes, while in 1945 Summerson contributed an essay on the architecture of Butterfield to the special Gothic Revival number of the magazine. But the work of that Victorian master could not be taken on its own terms; it may have become less of a joke, but it was still to be seen as something extreme and perverse, the architecture of protest.

> All Butterfield's churches are to a greater or lesser degree ugly. And in almost all there is a power and originality transcending the ugliness. . . The first glory of Butterfield is, to me, his utter ruthlessness. How he hated 'taste'! And how right he was![20]

In an essay on the criteria for preservation written after the war in 1947, Summerson could cite Victorians such as Butterfield, along with Cockerell and Pugin, among the great architects whose works deserved consideration although he advanced no case for Victorian buildings in general. And about the same time he could write of the 'wiser' Victorian architects who, by sticking closely to their chosen styles, 'produced some remarkable buildings which have an involuntary Victorian twist which we are beginning to find interesting'.[21]

Summerson was much involved with the growing preservation movement. He had been deputy director of the National Buildings Record, established in 1941 to record buildings threatened or damaged by enemy action (and had himself been taking photographs of certain remarkable Victorian Gothic churches before the war). He was also called on to advise on the statutory listing of historic buildings rendered possible by the 1944 Town & Country Planning Act and, perhaps surprisingly, found himself recommending a number of Victorian structures for protection. The advisory committee established for this purpose was not as prejudiced against more recent buildings as might be supposed and, as the

architectural historian Frank Kelsall has recently shown, no end date for listing was cited in the 'Instructions to Investigators'. Summerson and Goodhart-Rendel considered Victorian and even inter-war candidates on inspection tours in the latter's Rolls-Royce, and Rendel, much as he objected 'very violently to telling owners what they may not do with their own', argued that

> a spotlight must be turned on 19th century architecture soon in order to call attention to its beauties and to collect all willing collaboration that we can in avoiding their needless destruction.[22]

After the Second World War, a number of writers were beginning to take Victorian buildings seriously and pointing out their merits. John Betjeman, soon to become identified, often to his dismay, with a sentimental affection for all things Victorian, contributed an essay on Victorian Architecture (as well as ones on railway and Nonconformist buildings) to his collection *First and Last Loves*, published in 1952, but it may well have been his poetry as well as his newspaper articles which were the more influential in changing public opinion. Nikolaus Pevsner provided sober, if sometimes dismissive, assessments of notable Victorian works to the increasingly magisterial volumes of the *Buildings of England* series which began to appear in 1951, having moved on from an exclusive preoccupation with progressive tendencies in 19th-century design evident in his 1936 book, *Pioneers of the Modern Movement*.

Also in 1951, Pevsner gave a series of four BBC radio talks on Victorian Architecture, still feeling as an historian rather than as an enthusiast that there was 'an intrinsic deficiency in all Victorian architecture, a very real collapse in values'.[23] Meanwhile the American historian Henry-Russell Hitchcock (1903–87) was undertaking an exhaustive survey resulting in the publication of the two volumes of his study of *Early Victorian Architecture in Britain* in 1954.

Other authors continued to exhibit conventional prejudices, however, and to regard certain Victorian buildings as self-evidently ridiculous. One, in particular, was repeatedly selected to serve this

purpose. The wood engraving of Quar Wood in Gloucestershire, a grand Continental Gothic vicarage by J.L. Pearson, in C.L. Eastlake's *History of the Gothic Revival in England* was reproduced in 1954 in a book on *The Victorian Home* by Ralph Dutton, who commented, 'It seems unlikely that anyone will again share Eastlake's partiality for Quar Wood'.[24] The same illustration had already been reproduced in a book on *The Smaller English House* by Reginald Turnor as well as in Trevelyan's *Illustrated English Social History* – in both cases without dismissive remarks because comment was presumably deemed superfluous. No wonder, perhaps, that this intriguing building was mutilated out of recognition in 1954 in a vain attempt to make it look like an old Cotswold manor house. In a general history of *Nineteenth Century Architecture in Britain* published in 1950, Turnor could write:

> Most Victorian architects, of course, delighted in horrid materials, but Butterfield, with his craze for stripes of black and yellow brickwork against feverish red, outdid them all.

And,

> Even those critics who dislike good taste find it hard to praise Waterhouse for not having it; . . . he has failed to amuse anyone.[25]

Humour was not sought, however, in *An Introduction to Victorian Architecture*, a short, but fair-minded, well-illustrated book by the architect Hugh Casson, published in 1948.

Perhaps surprisingly, Casson – the committed modernist designer of the 1951 Festival of Britain –

◄ ▲ Quar Wood, Stow-on-the-Wold, Gloucestershire, by J.L. Pearson, 1857: engraving from the *History of the Gothic Revival* by C.L. Eastlake, 1872, and photograph of the house before it was mutilated by Sir Denys Colquhoun Flowerdew Lowson, Bt.

was one of the first to protest at the plan to demolish the Imperial Institute in South Kensington revealed in 1954 (see page 126). The British Government had decided that this great symbol of Empire and of Queen Victoria's reign, not Gothic but designed in an eclectic Renaissance manner by T.E. Collcutt in 1887 and paid for by public subscription within Britain and beyond, had to be sacrificed for new buildings for the Imperial College of Science. The Institute was not, wrote Casson:

> as it would-be destroyers would suggest, just another quaint old crock beloved by a few perverse 'Victoriamaniacs'. It is unquestionably a masterpiece, one of the finest buildings of its period not only in England but in Europe. To destroy it would be certainly an act of vandalism, and, to put it at its lowest, of extravagance as well.[26]

But this and other protests were of no avail and down it came – apart from the campanile.

Attitudes to Victorian architecture may have been slowly beginning to change, but by the middle of the 1950s, the architectural legacy of the Victorians was seriously threatened with destruction. Major Victorian monuments that once seemed so permanent appeared vulnerable but, given the prejudice against them held both by architects and so many in positions of authority,

◀ St Trinian's School imagined by Ronald Searle, from 'Timothy Shy', *The Terror of St Trinian's*, 1952.

perhaps it is surprising that so many still stood. The reason for this was, as the architectural historian Mark Girouard once pointed out, 'They survived for reasons of economics rather than of taste. Victorian buildings were relatively new, superbly solid, still in mint condition and mostly used for the purposes for which they had been built'.[27] So much of the built environment, not least working public buildings – government offices and town halls, university colleges and schools, railway stations and churches – were products of the Victorian decades so that it would have been prodigal to replace them merely because they were unfashionable.

Such major Victorian buildings as had already disappeared were almost all the victims of accident or enemy action (apart from country houses, which suffered, along with so many older and more respectable examples, from the changed economic and social conditions following the First World War, as well as from damage inflicted by the British during the Second World War after being requisitioned by the military). The most prominent casualty of accidental fire was, of course, that supreme symbol of the Victorian faith in progress and free trade, the Crystal Palace at Sydenham, which perished in 1936. Gilbert Scott's town hall at Preston also went up in flames in 1947. Many more fine Victorian buildings fell victim to bombs during the Second World War, notably Norman Shaw's New Zealand Chambers in the City of London, J.L. Pearson's magnificent brick-vaulted church in Red Lion Square and 'Greek' Thomson's extraordinary Queen's Park church in Glasgow. But it is also true that many buildings which were gutted and which could have been re-roofed and restored, such as Waterhouse's Assize Courts in Manchester and

Gilbert Scott junior's church in Kennington, were left open to the weather for a decade before being cleared away. Such Victorian masterpieces were, in the event, as much victims of anti-Victorian prejudice in the post-war years as of enemy action.

The 1950s saw the beginning of a difficult and dangerous period for Victorian architecture. Conventional taste had now caught up with blinkered intellectual opinion in dismissing it as hideous as well as old fashioned. It was not helped by the fact that, after six years of war followed by more of austerity, many Victorian buildings were dirty and neglected while so much sub-standard housing also dated from the 19th century. This was a legacy which politicians had committed themselves to sweeping away in favour of a bright, modern, clean, re-planned Britain. Now the nation geared for an orgy of long-planned comprehensive redevelopment while Modernism dominated the architectural profession with its indifference towards, or contempt for, the past. Its acolytes, smugly confident in their delusion that their favoured style was not a style, felt able to dismiss the Victorians for their creative dependence on history and for not having a style of their own –

◀ ▲ The interior of St Agnes' Church, Kennington Park, the masterpiece of George Gilbert Scott junior, looking west in c.1930 and in 1944.

▲ The ruins of Preston Town Hall by George Gilbert Scott, 1862–67, immediately after the fire which gutted it in March 1947.

failing to see that they had, in fact, made something new and distinctive out of the past.

By the late-1950s, town-planning schemes intended to deal with bomb-damaged or apparently outmoded cities were now being put into effect (and would wreak havoc in what were largely Victorian industrial cities like Bradford and Dundee). Britain had to be made fit for the motor car rather than the steam train. And this modernist-inspired utopianism was exacerbated by the boom in property

'All over the country the grime, muddle and decay of our Victorian heritage is being replaced and the quality of urban life uplifted!' – Harold Wilson. (5 October 1967)

◀ Pocket cartoon by Osbert Lancaster, from the *Daily Express* 1967.

development unleashed under the Conservative government of Harold Macmillan. The process continued, with immensely destructive effect, right through the 1960s and beyond. In 1967, the Labour Prime Minister Harold Wilson could claim that, 'All over the country the grime, muddle and decay of our Victorian heritage is being replaced and the quality of urban life uplifted!' (a fatuous observation immediately satirised in one of Osbert Lancaster's pocket cartoons).[28]

The case of Glasgow shows how malevolently destructive this climate of opinion could be, fuelled as it was by self-hatred as much as utopianism. Perceived as a Victorian city, both at its best and worst, Glasgow began to carry out long considered projects for urban renewal in the early 1960s. Great swathes of stone-built tenements were cleared for comprehensive development while an urban motorway was driven right through the city centre. No quarter was given by the authorities to any Victorian building that stood in the way of either, no matter how distinguished. For instance, the Caledonia Road Church was the widely admired masterpiece of the city's architect-hero, Alexander 'Greek' Thomson, but stood on the edge of the Gorbals, an area marked for total annihilation. In

1964, the planning convener announced that the two surviving churches by Thomson could not be retained and that, 'the time may come when we may have to consider putting up a plaque instead of retaining certain buildings'.[29]

The Caledonia Road Church had been acquired two years earlier by Glasgow Corporation, which allowed it to be vandalised and the lead stripped from the roof. As the building was not secured, it came as no surprise that it went on fire in 1965 and seemed doomed. Pevsner, on behalf of the Victorian Society, pleaded that, 'I ought to be believed if I say that the Caledonia Road Church and the St Vincent Street church are among the half-dozen architecturally most valuable churches of their date anywhere in the world. I think it would be a disgrace if Glasgow allowed them to go'. But it was probably the letter from America by Henry-Russell Hitchcock, published in the Glasgow *Herald*, arguing that, 'it is without question the most remarkable and the most distinguished ecclesiastical edifice of the high Victorian decades'[30] that stayed the clearance of the gutted shell, although the contiguous tenements also designed by Thomson were soon demolished. The following decade, similar threats emerged to several buildings by Glasgow's other local hero, C.R. Mackintosh, and although these were eventually spared – to become an essential part of the city's image and assets for its tourist industry – the Corporation succeeded in dismantling the celebrated Ingram Street Tearooms in 1971.

So it was that, all over Britain, not just areas of 19th-century terraced housing but magnificent examples of Victorian architecture began to disappear. In London, it was the threat to the Imperial Institute which alerted people to just how vulnerable they were. Other major Victorian buildings whose fate was sealed in the late 1950s included the Bishop's House in Birmingham by the great Pugin – one of the most remarkable and influential designs of the century – sacrificed for the city's inner ring road, and Eaton Hall in Cheshire, that substantial and costly pile by Waterhouse, which could have become the core of a new university.

Something had to be done to check such destructive waste. A new society was needed to

▲ The tenement in Hospital Street, Glasgow, adjacent to the Caledonia Road Church by Alexander 'Greek' Thomson, in 1963, nine years before it was demolished.

fight for the best buildings of the Victorians, just as the Georgian Group (of the Society for the Protection of Ancient Buildings) had been established in 1937 in response to the steady attrition of Georgian architecture in London and the unjustifiable loss of so many of the grand 'private palaces', the aristocratic town houses of the 18th century. The Georgian Group was, in fact, prepared to fight for fine Classical buildings dating from after 1837 but the Gothic Revival needed a defender. The result was the foundation of the Victorian Society in 1958.

The prime movers were Betjeman and Anne, Countess of Rosse, in whose Kensington Italianate house (18 Stafford Terrace: today open to the public) the two founding meetings were held. The founders included those, like Goodhart-Rendel and Pevsner, who had long been interested in protecting the best examples of Victorian architecture. There were several architectural writers involved, like Christopher Hussey and the young Mark Girouard, and a few architects, notably Sir Hugh Casson. Several of those present had been founders of the Georgian Group, 21 years earlier. The 3rd Viscount Esher, long an

▶ The Euston 'Arch' photographed by Herbert Felton in 1960 shortly before it was demolished.

active friend to conservation bodies, was chosen as chairman. At the first annual general meeting the following year, he told members:

> You will see that there is plenty to be done, if we had the power and the influence to do it. We are pioneers in a new field. Vandals, profiteers and town planners – I bracket the three together – are afraid to incur the displeasure of the S.P.A.B. or the Georgian Group. They know they have to have a good case, and that public disapproval inspired by these societies has to be very carefully avoided or disarmed. But at present, no one listens to what we say, and 'Oh, it's only Victorian' means that it can be ruthlessly destroyed. But it is exciting, I think, to be just in time to save what will be admired tomorrow.[11]

Given the state of public and ostensibly informed opinion towards Victorian architecture, the new society was careful not to appear extreme or ridiculous, and was concerned only to fight for the best. Its manifesto stated:

> The objects of the Society comprise the study and appreciation of Victorian architecture and associated arts with a view to the preservation of outstanding examples. Such study is an essential step towards discrimination between the thousands of buildings and other products of the Victorian and Edwardian ages. By no means all these are worthy of preservation but some of them are great works of art and some of them are landmarks in our architectural and artistic history. Almost all are insufficiently appreciated at present and for this reason are in danger of neglect and destruction.[32]

Even the very best was vulnerable; looking through the early annual reports of the Society, it is shocking to see what buildings were seriously threatened – great works of British architecture

◀ The Coal Exchange in the City of London being demolished in 1962.

which are now conventionally admired and taken for granted as being of importance and merit: Barry's Bridgewater House, Pugin's Scarisbrick Hall and, incredibly, the Oxford Museum.

Notoriously, the Society's career began with a series of defeats. All causes need a martyr, and the Victorian Society soon acquired one in the shape of the Euston Arch. The story of the unnecessary destruction of Philip Hardwick's great Doric propylaeum in front of Euston Station – earliest and grandest monument of the Railway Age – has often been told. In 1959, the British Transport Commission announced that it stood in the way of the long-overdue rebuilding of the station and had to go – along with the Great Hall and other interiors restored just a few years earlier, in 1953. The Society argued that the stones of the so-called 'Arch' could perfectly well be taken down and re-erected by the Euston Road – the solution accepted by the London Midland & Scottish Railway in

response to pressure from the nascent Georgian Group back in 1938.[33]

But rebuilding the Arch did not accord with the new forward-looking image sought by British Railways in response to the car-culture overwhelming Britain at the time, while few in authority could apparently see any merit in preserving such a monument. A smug leading article in *The Times* newspaper pronounced against saving the propylaeum despite the fact that its own architectural correspondent, J.M. Richards, was campaigning in its favour and would later describe the whole affair as the 'Euston Murder'.[34]

In the end, what sealed the fate of the Euston Arch was that no public body was prepared to foot the bill for moving it. The estimate was £190,000 which, as the Society pertinently observed, was 'rather less than the Treasury ungrudgingly paid out about the same time for the purchase of two indifferent Renoirs, which no one was threatening to destroy'.[35] As always in Britain, flat, movable art was more highly prized than three-dimensional, static-built creations. Ultimately the murderer was the Prime Minister, that cynical old Whig, Harold Macmillan. In late 1961, a deputation went to Downing Street. Richards recalled:

Macmillan listened – or I suppose he listened; he sat without moving with his eyes apparently closed. He asked no questions; in fact he said nothing except that he would consider the matter. A statement was issued later to the effect that the Government had decided not to intervene.[36]

The murder of the Euston Arch was neither forgotten nor forgiven. It ensured that the next time British Railways proposed to replace a great Victorian station – in 1966 with St Pancras and King's Cross – the proposals were defeated.

Soon after the loss of the Euston Arch came the scandal of the destruction of the Coal Exchange in the City of London. Designed by James Bunning with an extraordinary internal cast-iron rotunda, it had opened in 1849. In 1958, the Corporation of London decided to demolish it, ostensibly to allow for the widening of Lower Thames Street but also to redevelop much of the site. The Victorian Society protested, and argued that the Coal Exchange was a structure of international importance. It was described by Pevsner as, 'Among the twelve irreplaceable buildings of 19th century England' and by Henry-Russell Hitchcock as the 'Prime mid-century monument of iron and glass construction, not alone of Britain, but of the World', important as Henri Labrouste's Bibliothèque Ste Geneviève in Paris, while those supreme apostles of modernism, Walter Gropius and Siegfried Giedion, were wheeled in to state that it was, 'a landmark in the history of early iron construction, and its interior is of sufficient architectural and historic merit to warrant our sincere hope that it may yet be saved'.[37]

The Society also came up with practical proposals to modify the building to allow for the road widening and to have the rotunda re-erected elsewhere but all in vain. The Corporation was uncooperative and declined to allow any respite, one member of the Court of Common Council

typically remarking that, 'We cannot spend time on the preservation of a Victorian building'.[38] The Coal Exchange was demolished, with indecent haste, at the end of 1962; its site then remained empty for a decade.

A year later came another major threat to a major building – but this time the Victorian Society would eventually emerge victorious. At the end of 1963, Geoffrey Rippon, Minister of Public Buildings & Works, announced that he had decided to demolish the Foreign Office, that grand Classical pile by Sir Gilbert Scott and Matthew Digby Wyatt resulting from the most absurdly mismanaged of all 19th-century architectural competitions. 'Has Mr Rippon not noticed that Whitehall and the circumference of St James's Park form the ceremonial scenic centre of one of the great capitals of the world?' asked the Society.

From Buckingham Palace to just short of the Houses of Parliament, the buildings form a series of Classic designs, varying much in quality but generally consistent, and deliberately so. The Foreign Office . . . ranks high among these buildings. . . As [Christopher] Hussey has written: 'For a century the spectacular Italianate pile, thanks to Palmerston's inspired obstinacy, has played the visual role intended by Inigo Jones to be filled by Whitehall Palace in the centre of the historic square mile comprising Westminster and St James's. Seen from the park down the lake, the dramatic mass of black and white Portland stone enriched with countless statues composes one of the most grandly picturesque urban landscapes in the world'.[39]

That this can still be enjoyed today – if, thanks to stone cleaning, without that dramatic chiaroscuro – is tribute to the Victorian Society's increasing success in campaigning and changing public opinion. The Society went into action over the threat to the Foreign Office with some confidence, vigorously opposing the demolition proposal, presenting alternative plans for retaining parts of the Foreign Office building and calling for the treatment of Whitehall to be considered as a whole. Unfortunately, the result of this plea was the production of a comprehensive plan by Sir Leslie Martin and Colin Buchanan, *Whitehall: a Plan for the National and Government Centre*, published in 1965. This megalomaniac conception envisaged the demolition of every building south of Downing Street and Richmond Terrace (almost all Victorian or Edwardian), except for the original block of New Scotland Yard by Norman Shaw and Lanchester & Rickards' Central Hall. The New Palace of Westminster was also graciously permitted to survive, as was Westminster Abbey, but the Middlesex Guildhall in Parliament Square was to be replaced by a conference centre.

The following year, the Society gave evidence at a public enquiry into the Broad Sanctuary area, wisely emphasising 'the symbolic value in a centre of democracy of mingling ancient buildings and mixed uses with the bureaucratic afflatus of Government' and pointing out that, instead of building a new conference centre, the grand rooms in the Foreign Office could be used for that purpose.[40] In the end, the Foreign Office was saved by inertia and the parsimony of the Treasury. The demise of the Colonial Office and the amalgamation of the Foreign and Commonwealth Offices in 1968 delayed a final decision until the 1980s when, with

the building now listed at Grade I and standing in the Government Precinct Conservation Area, demolition was unthinkable.

Restoration and modernisation of the building began in 1984. In addition to revealing magnificent interiors long disfigured by partitions and false ceilings, this achieved 25% more usable accommodation 'all for considerably less than the cost of demolition and rebuilding', as the Foreign & Commonwealth Office's own official guide admits.[41] As so often refurbishment is a more economical as well as a more environmentally responsible course than replacement.

Meanwhile, in 1968, the government had announced the demolition of all the buildings on the east side of Whitehall south of Richmond Terrace – including New Scotland Yard (which even Leslie Martin would have spared) – so as to erect one huge new office block together with an extension to Parliament in Bridge Street. Now supported by other preservation and amenity societies, the Victorian Society campaigned against this and a public inquiry was held in 1970. Norman Shaw's masterpiece, already listed at Grade I, was eventually saved to be converted into accommodation for Members of Parliament. By 1973 the Society was able to report, with justifiable pride:

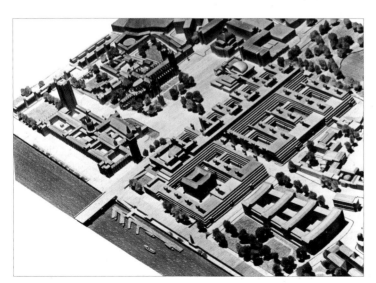

◀ The model showing the redevelopment of Whitehall and Parliament Square, from Sir Leslie Martin's report, *Whitehall: a Plan for the National and Government Centre*, 1965.

The reprieve of Whitehall represents, for us, a triumphant grand finale to nearly ten years of hard work. We have fought every inch of the way, round Parliament Square, from the Middlesex Guildhall, Sanctuary Buildings, the Central Hall, to the Palace of Westminster itself. Subsequently we fought for Whitehall: the Home Office, the Foreign Office, and last of all, for Scotland Yard, Richmond Terrace, and Parnell's Whitehall Club.[42]

Even so, these varied small-scale buildings in Whitehall remained threatened by subsequent government redevelopment schemes until the 1980s when more sensitive (and cheaper) proposals were carried out by William Whitfield. (Sad to add as a postscript that the Middlesex Guildhall has recently and unnecessarily been mutilated internally to make it the home of the Supreme Court.)

In 1973, the Victorian Society was 15 years old and triumphantly had achieved many of the aims of its founders. At long last, Victorian architecture was being taken seriously and valued. Big battles still had to be fought, of course, and many fine Victorian and Edwardian buildings would subsequently perish, including many churches – the following year Shaw's superb Holy Trinity Bingley would be blown up rather than repaired – but no major Victorian building of the calibre of the Euston Arch or the Coal Exchange would be lost.

If a single case is to be cited to mark the turn in public opinion which the 'Vic Soc' both encouraged and responded to, it must be that of St Pancras Station. In 1966, British Railways announced that the futures of both St Pancras and King's Cross Stations were under review. This was scarcely surprising: the Fat Controller, the egregious Dr Richard Beeching, had said that he hoped all the stations which survived his axe would be rebuilt. Just what was proposed was never explicit; either St Pancras would be closed and all the traffic diverted into its neighbour or vice versa with King's Cross becoming redundant. What was clear was that while the St Pancras train shed might become a museum or sports hall or whatever, British Railways was determined to demolish George Gilbert Scott's Midland Grand Hotel.

The Midland Grand had been closed in 1935 and it was probably only lack of funds that prevented its redevelopment before the Second World War.[43] King's Cross was now listed at Grade II while St Pancras was still only Grade III. However, public opinion was changing, perhaps mindful of the fate of the Euston Arch, so that British Railways' proposals provoked dismay, outrage and a great deal of controversy. The Victorian Society campaigned against demolition and demonstrated that Scott's building was perfectly capable of being modernised and brought back into use as an hotel and that the spectacular 243-ft span train shed by W.H. Barlow and R.M. Ordish, if made redundant, could and should serve a new purpose, such as becoming a national railway museum. Both, the Society insisted, were

indispensable masterpieces. In their romantic skyline, technical mastery and internal splendour they express the finest qualities of the greatest period of British history and imperatively require preservation.[44]

The apparently simple rationalism of King's Cross by Lewis Cubitt, 1851–52, had long been more highly regarded by modern-minded architects and critics than Scott's Gothic Revival extravaganza next door. The problem was that the High Victorian Gothic Revival – as younger members of the Vic Soc now called it – in general and the work of the famously, or notoriously, prolific Gilbert Scott in particular was still regarded as ridiculous by conventional taste. While Jack Simmons was at work on a monograph on the station, Betjeman did his best to educate people on the virtues of the Midland Hotel. 'The vaulted passages are like a cathedral, and the views from the windows are unexampled', he wrote in an article in a Sunday newspaper.

More damage has been done to London and our other old towns by 'developers' and their tame architects than ever was done by German bombing. No one can object to the clearance of what is shoddy and badly built. St Pancras Station is neither. . .[45]

◀ Back-to-back housing in Leeds, photographed in the 1960s.

Betjeman also tried to enlist the support of his old friend John Summerson.

'Have you come to admire, as K[enneth] Clark and I have, some of the work of Sir Gilbert, including St Pancras station, which is to be pulled down?' he wrote to 'Coolmore' in June 1966, in a letter which reveals the tensions among the protagonists over the new seriousness about Victorian architecture introduced by Pevsner.

> Would you be prepared to write an appreciative article on it? You count and I don't. It is no good writing about Sir Gilbert and St Pancras in particular, because I have been so denigrated by Karl Marx [i.e., J.M. Richards], and the Professor-Doktor [Pevsner] as a lightweight wax fruit merchant, I will not carry the necessary guns.

'No,' replied Summerson, typically fastidious and detached.

> I just couldn't put any heart into the idea of preserving it. . . Every time I look at the building I'm consumed with admiration in the cleverness of the detail and every time I leave it I wonder why as a whole it is so nauseating. . . I shall hate to see all that gorgeous detail being hacked down but I really don't think one could go to a Minister and say this is a great piece of architecture, a great national monument.[46]

Summerson, however, then changed his mind – possibly because he was then working on lectures to be published as *Victorian Architecture: Four Studies in Evaluation* – and he wrote what was introduced as a 'cool appraisal' of the arguments over St Pancras for the Illustrated London News the following year. Recalling when the building was still an hotel, he began by commenting on changing attitudes:

> We forget how deeply Victorian things – especially Victorian buildings – were hated in those days. St Pancras Hotel, in particular, was loathed for its size and pretension, its colour and ornamentation, and I think also for the obviously rather improper association of cathedral architecture with railway lines; for railways in those days were railways, not dear quaint old things. . . Today, with St Pancras Station and hotel in danger of dispersal and possibly demolition, a somewhat different attitude prevails. St Pancras, to a new generation, is glorious, unique, romantic, its skyline sheer poetry, its detail exquisite. St Pancras must be saved.[47]

In the event, the relevant Minister *was* persuaded that St Pancras was a great piece of architecture. What saved the station was it being listed at Grade I in October 1967, very much thanks to Lord Kennet (Wayland Young), Parliamentary Secretary to the

▶ Norman Shaw's Holy Trinity Church, Bingley, Yorkshire, being blown up, 7th April 1974.

Ministry of Housing & Local Government (and, that rare thing, a politician who was both civilized and a conservationist). The following year British Railways announced that St Pancras would remain in use. King's Cross was then improved by having the unsightly additions in front of the original twin-arched façade replaced by a newly designed unsightly addition, but British Railways merely sulked over St Pancras, allowing the former Midland Hotel to fall further into decay. A public inquiry had to be fought in 1980 to prevent the booking hall being further spoilt before the decision to make St Pancras the London terminus for high-speed Channel Tunnel trains allowed Scott's hotel to be restored and Barlow's train shed to be reborn – to ecstatic public acclaim – as St Pancras International Railway Station, capturing the imagination of the public as no modern station in Britain has done.

If ever the saving of a building justified the Victorian Society's existence it is surely this. In 2007, a statue of Sir John Betjeman was installed on the restored and converted St Pancras concourse as a tribute to his campaigning to preserve the building but in this case, in truth, Sir Nikolaus Pevsner, the second and most influential chairman, whose authority and gravitas so much strengthened the Victorian Society in the crucial years, deserved this doubtful accolade rather more.[48] As Lord Kennet concluded about Pevsner's achievement when he stepped down as chairman in 1976, 'It wasn't this or that building. He saved a whole century'.[49]

But even with Pevsner and Betjeman, the Victorian Society alone could not have changed public opinion. Indeed, the Victorian Society itself was a product of a wider sea change in attitudes towards the Victorians and this mainly took place in the 1960s, the decade more usually associated with the high tide of arrogant, destructive modernism. This slow change of mind manifested itself in such things as a growing number of books and other publications exploring Victorian themes, in exhibitions about Victorian painters (Madox Brown, Millais) and in films for both television and the cinema (*The Forsyte Saga*, Ken Russell's *Elgar* and *Rossetti*). Such films as *The Charge of the Light Brigade* expressed a delight in dressing up in Victorian uniforms, which also manifested itself in the contemporary record sleeve for the Beatles' *Sgt. Pepper's Lonely Hearts Club Band* album and in what was on sale in Carnaby Street and the Portobello Road market. There was also the Art Nouveau Revival, with exhibitions on Mucha and Beardsley, which made decoration and pattern respectable again and also influenced the contemporary dropout culture of decadence.[50]

And then came the beginning of the widespread reaction against modernist architecture encouraged by the partial collapse of the Ronan Point residential tower-block after a gas explosion in 1968. Now, in contrast to the new developments in so many cities, Victorian buildings seemed enjoyably colourful, decorative and solid – qualities which began to influence the design of some new housing developments. This change in attitude can be detected in the brilliant writings of Ian Nairn, who visited towns and cities all over Britain in the early 1960s, full of optimism for the future, but on his return in 1967 he became 'very much sadder about the prospects of a proper modern architecture, even more so about the capabilities of modern architects'. In Glasgow, for instance, he found that, 'There seems to be no break in the bland self-confident surface that doesn't care and doesn't want to care. This is true philistinism. . . Caledonia Road church is a burnt-out shell, waiting for some self-congratulatory act of demolition'.[51] At the same time, Nairn began to revel in the qualities of the toughest, most difficult High Victorian Gothic – above all, in the strange work of S.S. Teulon. St Mark's, Silvertown, in east London, he thought:

A hard punch right in the guts . . . Teulon's style has stopped being merely original, has become fused with glittering poetry, all knobbly with harsh polysyllables . . . Imploded, savage inward raids into the heart's essence, an architectural imagination the size of Blake's.[52]

As Betjeman observed, a few years later:

The only conquering force on the side of architectural preservation is affection for the buildings worth preserving. Taste changes, so that the foundation of the Victorian Society is considered by some elderly people as an unnecessary obstacle invented by intellectuals who like wax fruit and whatnots in the Portobello Road.[53]

The worst cases of the deliberate destruction of Victorian buildings occurred between the late 1950s – with the demolition of the Imperial Institute – and the mid-1970s – with the dynamiting of Norman Shaw's church at Bingley. Other fine and potentially useful examples of Victorian and Edwardian architecture would subsequently perish, of course, and two momentous public inquiries had to be fought in the 1980s to try, in vain, to preserve that unique concentration of mid-Victorian commercial buildings which stood next to the Mansion House in the City of London. But no major monument has been demolished (rather than simply been spoiled) in more recent decades.

Some building types have been and remain vulnerable, however. Hospitals and, above all, mental asylums – substantial, well-built and, in their own terms and time, enlightened pieces of design – together with their sites, have been squandered. Swimming pools, another expression of Victorian reformist and philanthropic impulses, continue to be closed and abandon, usually because local authorities decline to maintain them, while school buildings – especially Board Schools – remain vulnerable to current prodigal and misconceived government policies.

Public opinion has certainly changed. Victorian architecture is no longer mocked (although it is surely legitimate to find certain

▶ Hafodunos Hall, Clywd, by George Gilbert Scott, 1861–66, photographed in 1954; the housed was gutted by two young local arsonists in 2004 and now stands as a precarious ruin.

buildings and the pompous behaviour of certain Victorian architects funny – after all, the Victorians themselves would surely find it ludicrous that today we have given peerages to a pair of over-praised fashionable architects). No longer is there the dearth of scholarly writing about Victorian architecture of which Pevsner complained. Since the 1950s, the work of Victorian architects has been the subject of serious research and much has been published.

The old prejudices still linger, however. Notices attached to hoardings around the holes in the road that, at the time of writing, create chaos all over London announce that Thames Water is, 'Replacing London's Victorian water mains', explaining that, 'Over half the mains are at least 100 years old' when what, surely, deserves comment – and praise – is that the sewers and pipes laid down by Sir Joseph Bazalgette and other Victorian engineers were so well made that they have lasted such a long time despite poor maintenance. And when politicians smugly attempt to curry favour by announcing the replacement of Board Schools merely because they are Victorian, they might like to reflect that the children being educated in those solid,

adaptable buildings might be more fortunate than those using the cheap and insubstantial replacements of the latter half of the 20th century – especially as they share a privilege enjoyed by those who attend public schools with their wealth of fine Victorian buildings.

The photographs that follow illustrate examples of good Victorian architecture which, had they survived, would today mostly be admired, cherished and listed (though earlier listing failed to save some of them). Examples of Victorian terraced housing, which perished in their thousands, have not been included as, although often substantial and capable of refurbishment and improvement, they do not represent the higher ideals of Victorian architects. Besides, slum clearance was sometimes fully justified, although it is not necessary to agree with Robert Furneaux Jordan's absurd contention that, 'the main contribution of the Victorian Age to architecture is the Slum',[54] not least because the modernism promoted by his own generation did its best to compete.

The selection of buildings here cannot be offered as comprehensive. Several important Victorian country houses were illustrated in the *Country Life* archive volumes also published by

Aurum, notably Giles Worsley's *England's Lost Houses* and Ian Gow's *Scotland's Lost Houses*, while many lost urban buildings dating from the 19th century in cities such as Bradford, Dundee, Glasgow, Leeds, Liverpool and Manchester figure in the photographs reproduced in my own *Britain's Lost Cities*.

Some of the buildings illustrated here were eccentric rather than distinguished, but all were interesting and they include some of the very best examples of the creations of imaginative and resourceful Victorian architects. And all are buildings whose loss we may reasonably regret and which, if standing today, would be admired for their solidity, richness and confidence. After all, few would now agree with Harold Wilson that the 'quality of urban life' has been uplifted by replacing 'our Victorian heritage', for all too often solid Victorian buildings were replaced by cheap modernist structures, which have proved so inadequate and repellent that they themselves have since been replaced. In a distressing number of cases, the reasons for demolishing good examples of Victorian architecture have proved misconceived or mendacious. Half a century ago, Harry Goodhart-Rendel – 'the father of us all', that is, of all those who care about Victorian buildings – remarked:

> Nowadays, we feel a much greater obligation not to throw things away than people used to feel, because we are much less confident than they used to be of being able to replace them with things of equal value. Victorians did not feel at all like that. . . [55]

This feeling, what might be described as cultural pessimism, is something that conservationists usually dare not admit to, but it is surely as reasonable today as it was in 1958 – the year the Victorian Society was founded. At least there is now general recognition of the value of so many Victorian buildings, so there is all the more reason bitterly to regret how many have been needlessly and thoughtlessly lost.

1: IRON & GLASS

Some of the most inventive, useful and memorable structures built by the Victorians were wholly or partly made of iron and glass. Many have perished: railway station train sheds, covered markets, conservatories and such brilliant creations as the iron Rotunda of the Coal Exchange (see page 72). Perhaps the saddest loss of all is that of the CRYSTAL PALACE, that world-famous product of Victorian experiment and enterprise, especially as its destruction was accidental. The pre-fabricated structure of iron and glass, first proposed by Sir Joseph Paxton and constructed by the contractors Fox & Henderson, was originally erected for the Great Exhibition held in Hyde Park in 1851.

So successful and admired was it that Paxton formed a company to re-erect the building, half as large again, higher and with additional transepts, on the top of Sydenham Hill in south London. A prominent landmark, it was sheathed in 25 acres of glass. Opened in 1854, the enlarged Crystal Palace was soon flanked by water towers designed by the great engineer Isambard Kingdom Brunel to feed the fountains in the extensive grounds. The north transept was destroyed by fire in 1866 and not rebuilt, but otherwise, despite many vicissitudes, the Palace carried on into the 20th century, perhaps getting a little shabby and was used for all sorts of exhibitions and events: 'Dilapidated, a vast glass judgement-seat of dogs and brass bands, it remained an astounding building, demanding critical as well as focal readjustment'.[1]

In its last days, the fortunes of the Crystal Palace improved, its apparently pioneering structure of iron and glass attracting the admiration of modernist architects: it was the building Erich Mendelsohn asked to see when he first arrived in Britain in 1933 and Le Corbusier described it as the 'herald of a new age'. Then on the last night of November 1936, an accidental fire rapidly took hold of its timber floors and contents so that almost the whole structure was destroyed in a dreadful spectacle visible from miles around. That this great relic of the Victorian Age, this symbol of the 19th-century belief in free trade and progress, should have perished seemed ominous when the clouds of war were already gathering. A few years later, the surviving water towers were toppled lest they aided the navigation of German bombers. 'Let's Build Another One!' argued John Betjeman immediately after the fire.

◄◄ The Crystal Palace at Sydenham seen from the terraces and a distant view from the south in c.1860-66.

It is an emblem of all that was best in the great Victorian age, when England was prosperous and full of hope: when she was bolder than she is now. Remember, too, that though the Crystal Palace was built in 1851, it is still the most modern building in the country. There would be nothing sentimental in rebuilding this greatest of Victorian cathedrals.[2]

Alas, that did not happen, and probably could not – then. Even so, the Crystal Palace had an after-life. A photograph of its ruin was used as the frontispiece to the catalogue of the exhibition *Modern Architecture in England*, held at the Museum of Modern Art in New York the following year, and the semi-circular arched transept motif in metal and glass lives on, like the grin of the Cheshire cat, in dozens of shopping precincts built in recent decades. But nothing replaced the Palace itself on the top of Sydenham Hill and, following the destruction of associated buildings such as the High Level Station (see page 51), its magnificent site remains desolate, the most melancholy in London. Perhaps it really should be rebuilt now? It certainly could be.

Paxton's earlier iron and glass structures, precursors of the Crystal Palace, have also perished – but not by accident. These were the conservatories and glass-houses in the gardens at Chatsworth in Derbyshire, designed and built by Paxton for his employer, patron and friend, the 6th Duke of Devonshire. One was the Lily House, built in 1849–50 for the celebrated *Victoria Regia* lily. But the most spectacular was the GREAT CONSERVATORY, or 'Great Stove', constructed in 1836–40 with some assistance from the architect Decimus Burton. With its curved surfaces on laminated wooden beams supported on cast-iron

◀◀ The interior of the Crystal Palace in the 1860s.

▼ Joseph Paxton's 'Great Stove' at Chatsworth, Derbyshire, in the early 20th century.

◄◄ ▲ The Kirkgate Market in Bradford exterior in 1973; over the main entrance arch were figures of Pomona and Flora by William Day Keyworth.

columns and the use of the ridge-and-furrow system of glazing developed by Paxton, this was a remarkable and beautiful structure. With 40 miles of sash bars and measuring 277 x 123ft, it was also spectacularly large: the largest glass building in the world at the time. A carriage and pair could be driven down its central aisle.

The Duchess of Sutherland wrote, '. . . after St Peter's there is nothing like the Conservatory . . . the conception is so bold, the success so perfect'.[3] It was, however, an expensive luxury and in 1920, was removed by the 9th Duke of Devonshire (the same duke who disposed of Devonshire House in London the same year) – 'the solution to the problem of upkeep having been found in dynamite,' as Raymond McGrath and A.C. Frost put it.[4] In fact, five attempts to blow it up were made before the coup de grâce was delivered by Paxton's engineer grandson: Charles Markham. A rose garden was planted on the site.

Many Victorian public buildings were constructed wholly or partly of cast-iron and glass. This form of construction was found particularly suitable for markets, allowing for the creation of large, light and hygienic covered spaces within masonry walls. A particularly sad loss is that of the KIRKGATE MARKET in BRADFORD, not least because its removal was entirely unnecessary. The destruction of this popular local institution was all too typical of what was happening to fine buildings in many other cities at the time. Bradford was once a Victorian city, with a distinct character of its own. It expanded rapidly – too rapidly – in the 19th century to become the worsted textile capital of the world. A century later, in the 1960s and 1970s, its centre was systematically destroyed and far too many of its Victorian buildings, usually designed by local architects, were replaced by tawdry mediocrity.

The Bradford Markets were designed by the local firm of Lockwood & Mawson, architects of Bradford's Town Hall and Wool Exchange, and constructed in 1871–78. Unlike those buildings, the stone exterior of this large urban block on an awkward sloping site was Italianate Classical in style, enriched with fine sculpture by W.D. Keyworth. Inside, all was of richly decorated ironwork. Iron columns divided up the large internal area, creating aisles and large octagonal spaces covered by glass domes; more iron created

▶ The Kirkgate Market interior in 1973.

▼ The West Pier at Brighton, looking from the shore in 1970.

frontages for the perimeter shops, above which were high-level arched windows like elaborate fanlights. The iron was originally painted in a green and gold bronze colour. The Kirkgate Market flourished and was far from redundant when acquired by Town & City Properties, and Bradford was shocked when it was announced in 1973 that the whole building would be demolished to make way for an Arndale Centre. There was opposition, however – the loss of the Swan Arcade a decade earlier had not been forgotten or forgiven (see page 77). The Victorian Society protested, supported by two famous sons of Bradford – J.B. Priestley and David Hockney – and demonstrations against the market's destruction took place locally. But Bradford Council remained unmoved and the building came down that same year.

Its replacement 'is wholly without merit, massive concrete facing slabs and mean and badly arranged entrances obliterate the streetscape of Westgate and Kirkgate'.[5] This was designed by John Brunton & Partners, who afterwards said they regretted that the old market was not retained as part of the development – as well they might.

Lost examples of other buildings made partly of cast-iron are illustrated in other chapters, but one type of iron structure, quintessentially Victorian and yet peculiar and exotic, deserves mention here. This is the seaside pier. Many were built around the coast in the 19th and 20th centuries, usually of cast-iron but with timber used for the deck and the associated buildings.

And many have disappeared, often the victims of neglect, fire, storm damage or collisions with ships. One, in particular, can stand as both a representative and a supreme example: the WEST PIER at BRIGHTON. First constructed in 1863–66 and originally extending 1,115ft into the English Channel, this was the work of the doyen of Victorian pier engineers, Eugenius Birch. One pier historian describes it as 'Eugenius Birch's finest pier and, perhaps, considering its impact, the most important pier ever built. It was in the van of iron pier development, and set the standard for a generation of piers to follow'.[6]

The West Pier was extended in 1893 with a pavilion at its head, and its elaborate silhouette further enhanced by the construction of a large concert hall halfway along in 1916. In 1969 it was used for the filming of *Oh! What a Lovely War!* but two years later the seaward end was declared unsafe and the whole pier closed in 1975. But Brighton did not want to lose this hugely entertaining landmark and the West Pier Trust campaigned tirelessly for its restoration. In 1998, the Heritage Lottery Fund awarded £14 million towards restoring the pier, but the structure was badly damaged by storms in 2002. The following year, shortly after Brighton & Hove City Council gave permission for its restoration, the pier was set on fire by unidentified water-borne arsonists and its structure reduced to a forlorn mesh of twisted girders. So perished the loveliest of piers. Surprisingly, perhaps, no proper investigation into this crime, let alone any prosecution, has been made.

2: RAILWAYS

The Victorian Age was the Railway Age and some of the greatest and most characteristic buildings of the time were railway stations. 'Railway termini and hotels are to the nineteenth century what monasteries and cathedrals were to the thirteenth century,' observed *Building News* in 1875. 'They are truly the only representative buildings we possess'.[7] In the best of them, elaborate and decorative architecture in masonry was combined with iron and glass technology. Some were great urban termini – the 'cathedrals' – with vast iron and glass roofs over the platforms, but most were the small stations on main or branch lines, with modest masonry buildings housing ticket office and waiting rooms, perhaps Tudor or Gothic in style, combined with the platform canopies, with their iron columns and fretted timber valances – and a cast-iron footbridge over the railway tracks. Of these there were many hundreds.

The railway system, around which the Victorian economy and social life came to revolve, began with the opening of the Liverpool and Manchester Railway in 1830. It developed rapidly, by ruthless and frequent irresponsible private enterprise – often leading, it must be said, to the unnecessary duplication of lines and stations. By the time of Queen Victoria's death in 1901, Britain had almost 19,000 miles of working railway line, all with small stations along their length.

At first, it was unclear how the railway station would evolve in response to changing functional requirements. Early stations were designed to be harmonious with the landscape and to reassure passengers. Architects specialising in railway work emerged in the 1840s: William Tite, Francis Thompson and G.T. Andrews, for instance. By the 1850s the new technology of iron and glass was applied to larger stations. This reached its apogee (in Britain) in the 1860s with the creation of the vast, heroic single-span overall roofs – scarcely justified by economy or function – such as Cannon Street and, above all, St Pancras, where W.H. Barlow's train shed was the largest single span in the world. Although other large stations followed, such as Manchester Central and Glasgow St Enoch, later railway architecture in Britain was not so adventurous and less

◀◀ The Shareholders' Meeting Room at Euston Station following its restoration in 1953.

impressive. The other monumental structures required by the railway – the sublime tunnel entrances (usually Classical in style), the bridges and the great viaducts built on an heroic, Roman scale – should also be remembered, but these cannot be included here.

Most original railway buildings survived until the 1960s. Although the Big Four railway companies formed in 1923 modernised many stations, there were never the funds to rebuild the larger metropolitan ones. A project to rebuild Euston in 1938 was terminated by the Second World War, during which many stations were damaged but no major example destroyed. It was after the nationalisation of the railways in 1948, with their decline encouraged by the promotion of the car industry and the building of motorways, that devastating damage was done to the railway system and to Britain's remarkable railway heritage. Some closures were envisaged under British Railways' Modernisation Plan of 1955, but most followed the adoption of the report on *The Reshaping of British Railways* in 1963 by a Conservative government committed to a future based on road transport. This notorious decimation of the nation's railways is better known as the Beeching Plan – after the eponymous chairman of the British Transport Commission, appointed in 1961, who subsequently became chairman of the British Railways Board.

In 1961, there were still 17,800 miles of railway line in Britain, served by some 7,000 stations. Dr Beeching proposed closing 6,000 miles of line and some 3,000 stations, so that, by 1969, there were only 12,100 miles of railway still open. Even on the main lines that remained, intermediate stations were closed as stopping trains were withdrawn. Furthermore, the egregious 'Fat Controller' announced that he would like to see every working station rebuilt. Operating costs were all that mattered; passenger comfort – let alone architectural interest and historical importance – was not considered.

It may now seem astonishing that the great overall roofs of such stations as Glasgow Queen Street, Newcastle Central and Brighton, as well as Brunel's redundant train shed at Bristol Temple Meads, were then seriously threatened with demolition. Many stations were mutilated by the removal of their platform canopies and other features while others were simply allowed to decay before being replaced by crude glass shacks on windswept platforms – as if it was active policy to deter the public from using the railways.

The defeatist, bureaucratic vandals of British Railways did not have it all their own way, however. In 1964, the Victorian Society presented to the Ministries of Transport and Housing & Local Government a list of 60 stations 'specially worthy of preservation because of their architectural merit or historical interest'. And in 1967, after much controversy over the proposal to combine and rebuild St Pancras and King's Cross Stations, both were saved by the listing of the former at Grade I. A decade later, 481 railway structures were listed. Nevertheless, the attrition of fine and potentially re-usable railway buildings continued.

In the introduction to the catalogue of an exhibition about saving railway architecture, 'Off the Rails' mounted by SAVE Britain's Heritage in 1977, Simon Jenkins could write that:

> No group of British architects have had their work less cared for than railway architects. No aspect of British craftsmanship has been less conserved than that of our railway engineers. No land has been more extravagantly wasted or more disgracefully left unused than railway land – much of it in the central areas of our major cities.[8]

Two years later, in one of several books reflecting public interest in historic railway architecture, Marcus Binney claimed that British Rail, since nationalisation, 'has acquired for itself an all too deserved reputation as the biggest corporate vandal and iconoclast Britain has seen since the Tudor dissolution of the monasteries'.[9]

Matters have improved enormously since then, greatly assisted by the work of the Railways Heritage Trust, culminating in the triumphant restoration and adaptation of St Pancras as an international terminal. But it is depressing to contemplate how many fine railway buildings have been needlessly demolished – many of

which could have been used for other purposes and many more could still perform their original function on a revitalised railway system.

The most scandalous loss of a railway structure was, of course, that of the so-called EUSTON ARCH at EUSTON STATION, both because it was a monumental product of the heroic, pioneering phase of railway building as well as a superb expression of the Greek Revival, and because its destruction was unnecessary. John Summerson described it as a 'great museum piece commemorating as no other structure in the world the moment of supreme optimism in the marriage of steam and progress'.[10]

Not an arch but a propylaeum, it was built as the grand entrance to the London terminus of the first railway to the North, engineered by Robert Stephenson. It was designed by Philip Hardwick in the last days of the reign of William IV, but completed in 1838 in the first year of Queen Victoria's reign. Built of Bramley Fall stone, it had Doric columns 44ft high. 'Here was the gateway to the London & Birmingham Railway, one of the great achievements of man . . .' wrote Nikolaus Pevsner after its destruction. 'To celebrate it and then to commemorate it, only that style of architecture is worthy which stands in everyone's mind associatively for the greatest human achievement, the style of the Age of Pericles'.[11]

Originally, this extravagant entrance was flanked by lodges and stood at the end of a street leading north from Euston Square; it led to some comparatively modest buildings on one side with cast-iron canopies covering the platforms. The other half of the site had been intended for the Great Western Railway, but when that company pulled out and further accommodation was required, symmetry was abandoned. A GREAT HALL, or booking hall, and other offices were built to the west of the axis of the portico, designed in

▶ The Euston 'Arch' in 1934.

1846 by Hardwick's son, P.C. Hardwick, in an Italian Renaissance rather than a Greek manner. 'Never had there been and never has been since in England so magnificent a piece of railway architecture,' considered John Betjeman.[12]

The station subsequently developed around these structures in an incoherent and inconvenient way. It must be admitted that the London & North Western Railway did not treat the 'Arch' well. Further expansion removed one of its lodges while the vista from Euston Square was blocked by an hotel annex crossing the street, but the propylaeum remained a powerful landmark and symbol.

In 1938, to celebrate the centenary of the railway, the London Midland & Scottish Railway proposed a total rebuilding of the station, expanding it further south to Euston Square. This necessitated the removal of Hardwick's propylaeum, but the newly founded Georgian Group persuaded the company that it could be rebuilt further south on the Euston Road. This ambitious project was halted by the outbreak of

war in 1939. Then, in 1952, British Railways restored and redecorated both Hardwick's Great Hall and his Shareholders' Meeting Room.

In 1959, the British Transport Commission announced that Euston Station had to be rebuilt and enlarged as part of the plan to modernise and electrify the West Coast main line. Inevitably, the Great Hall and other buildings had to go, but the initial plans showed the Arch placed further south on the Euston Road. This idea was subsequently dropped. The London County Council and the Royal Fine Art Commission accepted the proposals provided the Arch was rebuilt elsewhere, but the LCC was supine and no authority prepared to pay the comparatively modest cost of re-erecting the structure.

Furious controversy raged for over a year, with the newly founded Victorian Society fighting vigorously for Hardwick's portico. Finally, a powerful deputation went to see an indifferent and philistine Prime Minister, Harold Macmillan, but in vain (see page 21). Demolition

work on the Arch began in October 1961. The contractor, Valori, later expressed surprise that he was not asked to number the stones for possible re-erection. The Great Hall and the rest of Euston Station were removed soon afterwards. An editorial in the *Architectural Review* the following year, written by J.M. Richards, which catalogued the sorry story of vacillation, prejudice, ignorance and parsimony resulting in demolition, was entitled 'The Euston Murder'. It concluded that:

'Just as the architects of the Rome railway terminus made something positive – and a visual asset – out of the idea of incorporating some ruined Roman walling in their modern complex of transparent walls and spaces, so the architects of the new Euston Station, given the will to find the perfect answer, not merely the easy way out, could have regarded this great arch as a challenge to produce a plan incorporating the old with the new and thereby showing it unnecessary to wipe out all of history whenever modernization is required.[13]

The replacement Euston Station, designed by R.L. Moorcroft, London Midland Region Architect, was completed in 1968. It is now proposed that this mediocre structure should itself be replaced

and the Euston Arch Trust is campaigning for the re-creation of the propylaeum.

The Euston portico exerted an influence down the line, with the Birmingham terminus of the railway (which still stands) designed by Hardwick in Greek Ionic. And in Glasgow, the first proper terminal station was, like the Euston Arch, in Greek Doric. This was GLASGOW BRIDGE STREET, opened in 1841. Designed by James Collie in 1839, its front in Bridge Street was dominated by a central tetrastyle Doric portico, surmounted by a pediment. This led to the offices and booking offices behind, whence staircases led to the platforms behind at high level. The station was extended in the 1880s after the railway had been continued north across the Clyde to Central Station. It was subsequently closed, but the noble Greek Revival portico lingered on until the 1950s, when it was mutilated, being finally demolished in 1971.

Many of the early stations were handsome Classical buildings, with some almost like country houses. NEWMARKET OLD STATION was a notably ornamental example. Designed by an unknown architect, it opened in 1848. With its large windows between pairs of projecting free-standing Ionic columns, it was a unique and beautiful curiosity – described by Christian Barman

▲ The portico entrance of Bridge Street Station in Glasgow in a mid-19th century photograph.

▲ Newmarket Old Station, photographed by F. J. Palmer in 1964.

as being like a 'Baroque orangery'.[14] The building was the terminus of a railway from Chesterford that was partly abandoned after only two years. It survived as a goods station after 1902, but by the time the Victorian Society campaigned for its preservation the stonework was fast decaying. After a public inquiry in 1968, a preservation order was placed on it, but the building was demolished during the following decade.

NINE ELMS STATION in Battersea was the original London terminus of the London & Southampton Railway. Opened in 1838, it was the third terminus to be built in the capital. Designed by Sir William Tite, architect of the Royal Exchange and of many early railway stations, it was an elegant Classical structure of brick and stucco with a central five-bay open arcade. Behind was a covered train shed with a timber roof supported on cast-iron columns and arched and pierced girders.

◀ William Tite's front to Nine Elms Station in Battersea, photographed by Sydney Newbery in 1942.

▶ The interior of Nine Elms
Station in 1942.

Nine Elms was by-passed in 1848 when the London & South Western Railway was extended to Waterloo. Tite's building was then used as a goods station but also for distinguished personages: Queen Victoria travelled to Osborne from the station until a special station was constructed for her a little further east, and Garibaldi alighted there to an enthusiastic reception in 1864. The station and its train shed survived intact until damaged by a bomb in 1944. Two years earlier, the building was recorded and one writer argued that, 'The old Nine Elms terminus is an extremely interesting survival and should be preserved. Here an important part of London's railway history began'.[15]

▶ The Great Western Hotel
at Snow Hill Station in
Birmingham in 1926.

In 1951, the British Transport Commission's Department of Historical Relics considered using Nine Elms as a transport museum, but the Southern Region of British Railways declined to release the building even though it had no plans for it and chose to neglect it. Eventually the museum opened in Clapham Common bus depot in 1961. After further mutilation, Tite's building was demolished in 1963 and the train shed soon after. A flower market, today redundant, was built on the site.

The Great Western Railway opened its own route to Birmingham in 1852 and built a station at SNOW HILL. By now, the railway companies promoted the building of hotels in association with important stations and the GREAT WESTERN HOTEL was built in 1863–69. Designed by the Birmingham architect J.A. Chatwin, its Italianate brick front faced Colmore Row and the churchyard of St Philip's Church, now the Cathedral. This was the finest hotel in the city when built, but in 1906 its upper floors were converted into railway offices. A plan by the G.W.R. was announced in 1938 to build a new hotel on the site, but was abandoned the following year with the outbreak of war.

In 1971, the Great Western Hotel was demolished during the orgy of redevelopment and road building in the city, which began in the late 1950s. The station behind, rebuilt in 1911–12, lost its main line services in 1967 and was finally demolished in 1976–77. However, the railway it served still runs through and under the city centre and a new smaller station was opened here in 1987. Now used by trains on the old G.W.R. route to London, this suggests the previous Snow Hill Station should never have been abandoned.

The London & North Western Railway also pushed a line through the centre of Birmingham, at huge expense, and built a large central station at NEW STREET in 1849–54 to replace its earlier terminus at Curzon Street. Originally named Grand Central Station, the platforms and tracks were covered by a magnificent single-span crescent-truss iron roof, 840ft long, whose maximum width at 212ft was the greatest in the world until St Pancras was built. It was designed by the engineer E.A. Cowper of Fox & Henderson, the firm that had built both the Crystal Palace and the train shed at Paddington. Because of the irregularly shaped site, no two trusses were the same length.

Designed by John Livock, the associated railway buildings principally consisted of the QUEEN'S

▸ The Queen's Hotel at
Birmingham New Street
Station in 1966.

HOTEL, whose Italianate frontage ran along Stephenson Street. Also opened in 1854, this was enlarged with additional floors and two towers in 1911. Then, in 1940, the great iron roof over the platforms was damaged by bombing and removed in 1948–52. The remainder of the old station, including the Queen's Hotel, was demolished in 1964–66, when the whole site was redeveloped. The station was then rebuilt. A shopping centre and office block of no architectural merit were built on top of a concrete raft placed over the platforms and railway tracks, making the revised New Street Station, with its minimal concourse, claustrophobic and thoroughly unpleasant to use. It is now proposed for another rebuilding.

London was comparatively unaffected by the physical presence of railways until the 1860s when, in a frenzy of building, new lines were thrust deep into and across the capital. Almost all of the resulting stations and lines survive in use, although some have been rebuilt, but one, BROAD STREET, has entirely disappeared. Broad Street was the terminus of the North London Railway and was built to connect the City of London with northern and western suburbs for commuter traffic. The line reached the City at high level on a viaduct from Dalston Junction. In 1865, the station building facing Liverpool Street opened and was apparently the work of William Baker, chief engineer of the London & North Western Railway, who engineered the line, although a lowly architect must surely have been involved.

Described as being in a 'mixed Italian style', the design was certainly eclectic, combining French Second Empire pavilion roofs with Ruskinian Lombardic round arches – notably in the open arcades on the steep side staircases climbing up from street to platform level. Soon after completion, Broad Street was joined by the new terminus of the Great Eastern Railway, Liverpool Street, next door. The front of Broad Street was spoilt by additional staircases and bridges placed within the iron entrance canopy in 1890–91, which were themselves replaced by a single-storey building in 1913.

In 1972, John Betjeman wrote that 'Broad Street is the saddest of all London stations. It has fallen greatness'.[16] By that time the twin span-iron train shed had been cut back, in 1967–68, leaving the platforms exposed and windswept. Wartime damage had never been repaired and now it was forlorn and neglected, its site ripe for

◄ The North London Railway's terminus at Broad Street in the City of London: photographed by Alex Starkey in c.1980.

lucrative commercial redevelopment. In 1975, British Rail announced plans to rebuild Liverpool Street Station with office accommodation over the platforms and to abolish Broad Street altogether, diverting the few trains that used it into Liverpool Street by a longer, circuitous route. The Greater London Council, the Victorian Society and SAVE Britain's Heritage objected.

Following a public inquiry held in 1976–77, most of Liverpool Street was reprieved, but Broad Street received sentence of death. The earlier, western train shed at Liverpool Street was retained and the station sensitively altered and extended in 1985–91. The demolition of Broad Street began in 1985 and its site together with that of the adjacent goods station used by the developers Rosehaugh Stanhope for their Broadgate Development. Today the surviving, abandoned viaduct north of the station is being annexed by the extension of the East London Line, which suggests that while the removal of Broad Street may have been commercially opportune, it did not benefit the travelling public.

It was also in the 1860s that the South Eastern Railway invaded central London from across the Thames, extending its lines from London Bridge

▼ The arcaded staircase to the platforms at Broad Street in 1976.

Cannon Street Station in the 1950s, seen from the south side of the railway bridge across the Thames.

to vast new termini at Charing Cross and Cannon Street. At Charing Cross, the original arched shed roof collapsed in 1905 and the station now finds itself underneath a large commercial block, Embankment Place, but the Charing Cross Hotel survives, although its top floors and roof have been mutilated.

CANNON STREET STATION was finer. Designed by the engineers John Hawkshaw and John Wolfe Barry and opened in 1866, the platforms were raised above vaults and covered by a wide arched train shed, 190ft in span, facing the river. This splendid roof was contained within vast brick walls terminated by the Thames in towers topped with domes and spires, as if to echo the form of the surviving steeples of Wren's City Churches nearby. 'Full of the pride of the late eighteen-sixties,' wrote the railway historian Hamilton Ellis, 'the South Eastern's terminus at Cannon Street was one of the finest structures on Thames side'.[17]

The Cannon Street Station Hotel in c.1867.

◁ Crystal Palace High Level Station from the north-west in the 1950s following its closure.

At the landward end of the station was The CANNON STREET HOTEL, built by an independent company. Opened in 1867 as the City Terminus Hotel, it was designed – like the Charing Cross Hotel – by Sir Charles Barry's second architect son, Edward Middleton Barry, in a dense Classical manner with spires enhancing the pavilion roofs. In 1931, the building was closed as an hotel and made into offices, renamed Southern House. Betjeman wrote of Cannon Street in 1952 that, 'Of all the stations of London it is my favourite, so echoing, so lofty and sad. Whoever used it and who uses it now?'[18]

The station had been hit by bombs in 1941, when the former hotel was burned out. All the glass was removed from the damaged train shed roof, eventually taken down in 1958–59. Thanks to representations from the Royal Fine Art Commission and others, the river end of the flanking brick walls, together with the towers, were retained. Southern House, reconstructed after the war, was demolished in 1963 as unsafe. It was replaced by a nondescript modern office block designed by the firm of the criminal architect John Poulson, who had useful connections with the British Railways property board. This has been

since replaced. Many commuters still use Cannon Street Station, but only the riverside towers suggest its former grandeur and glory.

Among suburban Victorian stations outside central London, the saddest loss must be that of CRYSTAL PALACE HIGH LEVEL because of its architectural distinction. The fortunes of this station were closely linked to those of Paxton's adjacent creation, although it managed to outlive the Crystal Palace by a quarter of a century. A railway was promoted by the London, Chatham & Dover Railway to cater for the crowds expected to visit the Crystal Palace. The line, which climbed up from Peckham Rye almost to the top of Sydenham Hill, opened in 1865 (and was painted soon afterwards by Camille Pissarro where it crossed Lordship Lane).

Trains emerged from a tunnel into a brick-lined cutting along the west side of Crystal Palace Parade parallel with the Palace. The terminus was at the southern end. Known as the High Level station to distinguish it from the London, Brighton & South Coast's earlier station further down the hill which opened in 1854, the building was designed by Edward Middleton Barry and was of considerable ambition. At either end of long covered platforms separated by a tall brick

▲ The interior of Crystal Palace High Level Station in the early 20th century.

▲ The entrance front of Crystal Palace High Level Station in Farquhar Road photographed in the late 1950s by John L. Smith (perspective corrected).

arcade were red-brick frontages with corner towers topped by four square turrets, with the architect's favourite French pavilion roofs. At the southern, entrance end in Farquhar Road, staircases led down to the platforms below.

Like the Crystal Palace itself, the High Level line never did quite as well as its promoters had hoped, and after the destruction of the Palace in 1936, passenger numbers dropped further. Despite the fact that the line had been electrified in 1925, it was closed in 1954. Damaged in the Second World War, the station lingered on until 1961, when it was cleared. Undistinguished housing was eventually built on the site. Had the railway survived, it would surely be a busy commuter route now. As it is, the absence of the railway and the station adds to the forlorn melancholy character of the top of Sydenham Hill. The High Level station was the principal passive victim of the 1936 fire, as many of the fine villas

built nearby on the Dulwich Estate also suffered neglect and then demolition (see page 169). All that survives today to speak of past glories (apart from the damaged, but extant and operating Low Level Station) is the decorative vaulted pedestrian passage under Crystal Palace Parade, which enabled arriving first-class ticket holders to reach Paxton's Palace directly from the High Level Station.

BRADFORD EXCHANGE was one of two proud railway termini serving the Yorkshire wool town; the other was Forster Square. Their fate, along with that of most of the city centre, was horribly representative of the most destructive and prodigal of attitudes towards the Victorian past. A joint station serving the Great Northern and Lancashire & Yorkshire Railways to the south of the centre, it was rebuilt and enlarged in 1888. The station had little visible presence outside; its glory was the twin arched iron train sheds, 450ft

▶ The train shed at Bradford Exchange Station being demolished in 1976.

▲ The interior of the northern train shed at St Enoch Station in Glasgow in 1975.

▲ The St Enoch Hotel in Glasgow in 1975.

long, each with a span of 100ft. Deemed too large, it was closed in 1973 and replaced by a smaller, far less impressive station much further to the south, just as the railway into Forster Square Station was cut back and a new terminus, consisting of a couple of miserable, tawdry platforms, built further north. It was all part of the comprehensive redevelopment of the city centre: a vision for the future that extolled the motor car and had no consideration for railways or the convenience of passengers. Bradford Exchange Station was demolished in 1976, along with the fine warehouses that stood in front of it. Its site is now occupied by a County Court.

Neither Bradford station was functionally redundant. GLASGOW ST ENOCH was redundant, yet its destruction even more foolish. Opened in 1876, St Enoch was the proud terminus of the Glasgow & South Western Railway which, as the City of Glasgow Union Railway, had smashed its way over the Clyde and into the city centre at huge cost. As the company was allied to the Midland Railway, the great train shed – like Manchester Central – bore a family resemblance to St Pancras. Designed by the distinguished engineer Sir John Fowler, assisted by J.F. Blair, it had a span of 204ft. Later, in 1898, the station was extended to the south with a smaller arched shed with a span of 140ft. In front, facing St Enoch Square, the company built the ST ENOCH HOTEL.

Designed by Thomas Willson of London, assisted by the local architect Miles S. Gibson, this was the largest hotel in Scotland when it opened in 1879, although it remained incomplete on the south side. For a time, the station and hotel flourished, with the Midland Railway's Scottish Pullman expresses travelling between saints: from St Pancras to St Enoch. But by the mid-20th century, with the nationalisation and rationalisation of the railway system, it made no sense for Glasgow to have four separate city-centre termini. St Enoch Station was closed in 1966; the hotel carried on until 1974 when it was also closed, ostensibly because it failed to comply with new fire regulations.

For a while, the magnificent train shed was used as a car park. It could have been converted into a conference and exhibition facility, as happened with Manchester Central, but it was demolished instead, in 1975. The hotel followed two years later, with the City Council claiming the site had been earmarked for offices for the Ministry of Defence – in the event, a very large greenhouse, containing a shopping centre of no architectural merit, replaced the station. Meanwhile, new hotels were built elsewhere in the city while a conference centre was constructed on an inconvenient and inaccessible site further down the Clyde. The extinction of St Enoch therefore seems an incomprehensibly foolish waste of a solidly built, well sited and potentially useful asset to Glasgow, but one that is by no means unique in that city.

It cannot be denied that some cities had too many terminal railway stations, each built by a separate company to serve different lines. In

▲▶ The exterior and interior of the booking hall at Birkenhead Woodside Station in 1967.

Liverpool, post-Beeching rationalisation and the construction of a linking underground loop saw the end of Liverpool Central and Liverpool Exchange. It also ensured the closure of BIRKENHEAD WOODSIDE. Built as the new terminus of a joint line through the Wirral peninsular, which allowed the Great Western to reach the Mersey and opened in 1878, Woodside was sited right next to the ferry terminal for Liverpool and was, effectively, another station serving that city.

Woodside had twin arched train sheds designed by the engineer E.W. Ives, but its glory was a great Gothic booking hall with an open timber roof. All the masonry buildings here were designed by R.E. Johnson rather in the manner of St Pancras. Birkenhead Woodside remained busy until its services were diverted into other stations and what is now the Merseyrail network. It closed in 1969 and

was demolished soon afterwards; no attempt was made to find another use for the (unlisted) buildings.

The self-defeating absurdity of the duplication of railway lines and stations resulting from private enterprise was well demonstrated in DUNDEE. Any passenger coming from Perth on the Caledonian Railway wanting to travel on eastwards would have to alight at Dundee West Station and walk to Dundee East, the terminus of the Dundee & Arbroath Railway. A railway through the docks connecting both lines by-passed the two stations, and it is on this line that the present through station for Dundee stands, on the site of the former North British Railway's Tay Bridge Station.

DUNDEE WEST was a terminus. It was rebuilt in 1888–89 with a grand Scottish Baronial building. This was apparently designed by John (or Thomas) Morrison Barr, the Caledonian Railway's district

▶ Dundee West Station, the terminus of the Caledonian Railway, photographed by Alexander Wilson in c.1890.

engineer in Perth, although the drawings were made by E.C. Moon. The clock tower was clearly modelled on the municipal buildings at Aberdeen designed by Peddie & Kinnear. Dundee East closed in 1959; Dundee West followed in 1965. Along with the extraordinary Royal Arch by the docks, it was demolished soon afterwards for new roads connected with the Tay Road Bridge.

Although the heroic period of railway station building in Britain was over before the end of Victoria's reign, railway construction continued with the threat represented by the advent of the internal combustion engine not being recognised at first.

In 1894, the Manchester, Sheffield & Lincolnshire Railway, now renamed the Great Central Railway, began work on its own main line to London, which opened in 1899. Its modest terminus at Marylebone survives; other stations on the route have perished. The grandest was NOTTINGHAM VICTORIA, a joint venture with the Great Northern Railway. It was built in 1898–1900, after three years and a fortune had been spent in acquiring its central site, requiring the demolition of some 1,300 houses. As at Marylebone, the train shed was utilitarian, but the station building was impressive and attempted magnificence. Built of red brick and stone in a free Renaissance style, it was designed by A.E. Lambert, the architect of the later – and surviving – Midland Station.

Unfortunately, some of the last railways to be built were the first to go: Nottingham Victoria was closed in 1967, its site and the adjacent railway cutting filled by the Victoria Centre comprising multi-storey car parks, blocks of flats and an indoor shopping centre. Only Lambert's clock tower survives. The loss is not just Nottingham's.

The Great Central main line was superbly engineered for high-speed running and built to accommodate wider trains on a Continental-loading gauge. This was because the megalomaniac railway promoter, Sir Edward Watkin, had a vision of his line connecting with the projected Channel Tunnel. In the event, that tunnel took another century to realise but had the Great Central main line survived, it would have provided a ready-made link for Continental traffic between the Midlands and the new railway from London to the France. Yet again, the enthusiasm for closure, abandonment and destruction in Britain proved shortsighted and ultimately very costly.

The same blinkered abandonment of expensive and potentially useful infrastructure occurred in Glasgow, inevitably, where much of the Glasgow Central Railway – opened in 1896 – was closed in 1964. Most of this railway ran underground and connected Central Station with north-western suburbs. The stations along the line were designed

▶ Botanic Gardens station in
Glasgow, photographed by
John R. Hume in 1966.

by two of Glasgow's celebrated *fin-de-siècle*
architects, J.J. Burnet and James Miller. The most
remarkable was BOTANIC GARDENS. The railway
tunnel ran right underneath these gardens, whose
owners – the Glasgow Botanic Institution –
insisted that station building be 'of such
ornamental character as will harmonise with the
surroundings thereof and to the satisfaction of
the Corporation and of the President of the said
Institution'.[19] In consequence, James Miller
created an exotic little building on the corner of
Great Western Road, which made a worthy
neighbour to Glasgow's famous conservatory, the
Kibble Palace. Like his later structures for the
1901 Glasgow International Exhibition, Miller's
station was fantastic: at once Tudor, Classical, Art
Nouveau and somehow Oriental in style; in 1898
the *Builder* described it thus:

> a pretty little red brick tiled building, with
> white woodwork and half-timbered gables, a
> strange sight in Glasgow; it has two tall turrets

on the roof with gilded onion-shaped domes, it
is very well grouped and detailed, and looks
too good architecturally for what it is.[20]

The steam-hauled railway suffered from the
competition of Glasgow's tram system and the
station was closed in 1939 on the outbreak of war,
never to reopen. Ground-level buildings were made
into shops and a café. In 1970, the roof was
damaged by fire. Glasgow Corporation then decided
not to repair it, no doubt as it was then
contemplating the widening of Great Western Road
as a dual-carriageway, so the city lost yet another
fine and enjoyable building. Today, the site of the
station remains derelict. Fortunately, Miller's
masterpiece for the Caledonian Railway, the station
down the Clyde at Wemyss Bay, survives.

Following the adoption of the Beeching Plan,
hundreds of small stations both on main lines and
on abandoned rural branch lines were closed. These
were the stations that made the Victorian railway
system so comprehensive and efficient. For them, a

◀ Midhurst Station in Sussex, with a LB&SCR locomotive of 1876 designed by William Stroudley, in c.1900-01.

distinctive pattern developed, with a cast-iron footbridge over the tracks and platform canopies, with iron columns – often with ornamental brackets – and a fretted timber valance, attached to the station buildings. The buildings themselves were often Tudor in style, giving the station a harmonious countrified character.

Such buildings, after closure, could easily have been used for other purposes. Some survivors became houses, but many other charming, well-built Victorian structures needlessly destroyed. Just one rural station has been selected here to represent these many, many lost railway buildings. The station at MIDHURST in Sussex replaced an earlier station in 1881, when the London, Brighton & South Coast Railway opened a line across the South Downs to Chichester. It was designed by T.H. Myres, a Preston architect who created a number of stations for the LB&SCR in the 'Old English' Domestic Revival style of Norman Shaw.

Midhurst was typical with decorative sunflowers incised into the cement infill to the half-timbering, tile-hanging and oriel windows. It also had a fine timber signal box on the platform as well as typical platform canopies. The station was closed to passengers in 1955 and the line finally closed in 1964. Five years later, the station was demolished and the site is now covered by a housing estate. Surely Myres's cottage-like building would have made a fine house?

3: HOTELS & BUILDINGS FOR PLEASURE

Several of the important urban stations mentioned above were associated with hotels. Some railway hotels stood alone in their magnificence and quality. One such was the HOLBORN VIADUCT HOTEL, which stood on the approach to Holborn Viaduct in front of the London Chatham & Dover's unimpressive station. A grand Classical building with a French pavilion roof, it looked as if it was intended to front a boulevard in Napoleon III's Paris.

Designed by Lewis H. Isaacs, the building opened in 1877. The splendid dining room was embellished with coats of arms of the towns served by the railway, but the enterprise was let to the railway caterers, Spiers & Pond. During the Great War, in 1917, the hotel was requisitioned by the government and eventually became the headquarters of the Henley Telegraph Works Company, although the ground floor refreshment rooms remained open until 1941. The Holborn Viaduct Hotel was badly damaged by bombs in

44 The Holborn Viaduct Hotel: the exterior when new photographed by Newton & Co. and the dining room as recorded by Bedford Lemere.

1941 and subsequently demolished. Its replacement was unworthy; John Betjeman considered that,

> No office blocks in the City are quite so dull as those which have replaced the hotels of Cannon Street and Holborn Viaduct. It is hard to believe that any consideration, other than finance, has guided their perpetrators. The human element is missing.[21]

Both have since been replaced.

Some hotels – like those in the City of London – failed to flourish as they were in the wrong place when newer and smarter hotels were built in the West End. Standards of luxury and comfort changed rapidly in the later 19th century and many hotels were eventually closed because they lacked sufficient bathrooms – an important consideration once Americans began to visit London in large numbers towards the end of Victoria's reign. But some were victims of fashion, of changing ideas about what was considered smart and glamorous. It was to that that the amazingly exotic and colourful IMPERIAL HOTEL ultimately fell victim.

The east side of Russell Square in Bloomsbury was once dominated by two astonishingly eclectic

▶ ▼ The extraordinary façade of the Imperial Hotel in Russell Square in 1966 and a view of the main lounge.

fin-de-siècle hotels, which were designed by Charles Fitzroy Doll, surveyor to the Bedford Estate. First, in 1898, came the Russell Hotel, a confection of gables, turrets and balconies inspired by François-Premier château architecture but carried out in glazed terra-cotta. In 1905–11 came its southern neighbour, the Imperial. Here, Doll went further, combining terra-cotta with red brick to make fantastic towers rise above a high mansard roof of green copper. In 1952, Nikolaus Pevsner wrote how the Imperial was,

> equally colossal but of a much more vicious mixture of Art Nouveau Gothic and Art Nouveau Tudor . . . We may well laugh at such exuberance. But is it not perhaps to be preferred for hotel architecture to the deadly eighty-four-bay barracks-frontage of the Royal Hotel in Woburn Place?

(since replaced by a bigger, but equally nondescript barracks).[22]

Alas, the Imperial Hotel was demolished in 1966, partly because of a lack of bathrooms but also because, according to the Greater London Council, 'the whole frame was so structurally unsound that there was no possibility of saving it if a preservation order had been placed on the building'.[23] In truth, however, the building was probably a victim of taste less developed and less accommodating than Pevsner's: it has since been replaced by a modern hotel wretched and mean in comparison to the Russell Hotel – mercifully this managed to survive and flourish.

But it was not just in London where exuberant Victorian hotel buildings fell victim to prejudice. In NOTTINGHAM once stood the BLACK BOY HOTEL, one of the finest creations of the local Nottinghamshire architect Fothergill Watson (who confusingly swapped his names around in 1892 to become Watson Fothergill). Fothergill Watson was architect to the Brunts' Charity, which owned the hotel in Long Row; he extended it in 1878 and then, in two building campaigns of 1887 and 1897, he rebuilt and enlarged the main front of the building.

The new work was all in the architect's characteristic combination of heavy,

▲ The Black Boy Hotel in Long Row in Nottingham, photographed by Ken Brand in 1963.

polychromatic Gothic in red brick and stone, and the gables and timberwork of Norman Shaw's 'Old English' manner. He maintained the traditional Nottingham colonnaded covered way at ground level while the upper parts of the hotel were enlivened with oriel windows, projecting timber gables and a brick tower. The Black Boy was demolished in 1970; its replacement is miserable and unworthy.

Smart hotels also provided restaurants (where, by the end of the century, women could dine without impropriety), but Victorian London was also well served with large restaurants, often containing several dining rooms. Many of these once-famous establishments have gone. As the historian Hermione Hobhouse has observed,

▶ The Holborn Restaurant on the corner of Kingsway and High Holborn photographed by Bedford Lemere in 1935.

Restaurants are even more subject to the tide of fashion than hotels, dependent like all questions of fashion on the likings and habits of the class and age-group with most money available.[24]

One of the most architecturally ambitious, as well as being one of the largest establishments, was the HOLBORN RESTAURANT on the corner of High Holborn and Kingsway. A restaurant opened here in 1874, the site having been previously used for a casino, a swimming bath and then a dance-hall. It was rebuilt in 1883–85 by Archer & Green, the architects of Whitehall Court. In 1888, it was described as:

"recently reconstructed and palatial" and a place where dinner, "a judicious mixture of the French and English styles of cookery, is served daily from 5.30 to 8.30, and the diner has, besides an excellent meal, the opportunity of listening to a selection of first-class instrumental music, which is performed during the *table d'hôte* hours by an efficient band.[25]

In 1894–96, the Holborn Restaurant became even more palatial when T.E. Collcutt added an extension containing the King's Room, with murals by Gerald Moira. The Empire Grill Room was embellished with majolica and mosaic by Doulton's. At the height of its glory, the Holborn Restaurant contained 14 restaurants and private dining rooms, as well as three Masonic temples. All this was abandoned in 1955; at the demolition sale, 1,000 chairs and much else were on offer.

Like the hotel and the restaurant, the theatre developed into a sophisticated and richly ornamental building type towards the end of the 19th century. The architecture of the traditional theatre converged with that of the music hall or palace of varieties and the result was a boom in theatre building all over Britain in the Late Victorian and Edwardian decades. Several specialist architects emerged, adept at dealing with increasingly rigorous regulations to create richly decorated and comfortable auditoria, often on confined or awkward sites. There was C.J. Phipps, W.G.R. Sprague, Bertie Crewe and Ernest Runtz, but Frank Matcham was the doyen of theatre architects. 'Matchless Matcham' displayed genius in his ability to design large and gorgeously appointed auditoria with good sight lines, together with all the other necessary facilities and spaces, on difficult urban sites. Altogether, he built or transformed over 120 theatres.

Many of the theatres Matcham and his followers created, mostly in the 1890s, survive in

◀ The partly dismantled auditorium of the Metropolitan Theatre in the Edgware Road in 1963.

happy use today, but a huge number have been swept away. In *Curtains!!!, or, A New Life for Old Theatres*, published in 1982, it was estimated 85% of the 1,000 or so theatres standing in Britain had been demolished or irretrievably mutilated in what the theatre historian John Earl described as 'the great theatre massacre'.

> After the Second World War with cinema, and later television, seducing once-loyal audiences, theatre doors closed everywhere. Retreat became a rout, the axe falling not where society had judged that pruning and careful renewal might be advisable, but where developers' economics dictated. The best theatres on prime sites were often the first to go, but even in suburbs where development pressure was low demolition was almost the rule, a cleansing act of destruction being seen as a sort of passport to progress.[26]

Few of these buildings were protected by listing, a state of affairs which reflected architectural snobbery: theatre architecture was not taken very seriously and the great Victorian theatre architects, in their day, were not numbered among the recognised leaders of their profession.

The fate of the METROPOLITAN THEATRE in the EDGWARE ROAD, Paddington, was all too typical. It began as a music hall in 1862, but was rebuilt and transformed in 1897 by Frank Matcham as a palace of varieties with a 1,800 seats. As with most of Matcham's theatres, it was the atmosphere created within the complex hexagonal geometry of the auditorium that mattered. 'The Metropolitan provided to the very end a wealth of visual experiences which no drawing or still photograph can effectively convey,' John Earl later recalled.

> However one approached it, the first view of its glowing, nicotine-browned auditorium was immensely exciting. Its generously curving lines and sensuously detailed plasterwork gave no hint of the fact that it was (at least in part) new flesh on old bones. It was the work of a theatre master.

The Metropolitan was demolished in 1963.

> It stood in the path of an urban motorway whose completion was essential to the survival of the capital. No other alignment was possible. The theatre came down and the most environmentally damaging road in London [Westway] was eventually built – on a different alignment.[27]

◀ ▲ The awkwardly shaped exterior of the Granville Theatre of Varieties at Walham Green and two views of the auditorium photographed by Alfred Cracknell for the Architectural Press in 1949.

It was the destruction of another theatre in west London designed by Matcham which at long last encouraged the authorities to take Victorian theatre architecture seriously. The GRANVILLE THEATRE OF VARIETIES in WALHAM GREEN was designed and built (as usual, in a remarkably short space of time) on an awkward site in 1898. The exterior – with two 'minarets' marking the entrance on an acute corner – was not particularly successful, but the interior was spectacular.

At a stone-laying ceremony, one of the promoting company's directors, the comedian Dan Leno, raised a laugh by referring to 'these sanitary varieties'. This was because the auditorium was faced throughout with glazed Doulton faience: the balcony and box fronts, the proscenium arch and even the ceiling all covered in coloured and moulded ceramic. After the Second World War it could be said that,

there are few theatres in the great West End of London which can boast a more varied and exciting career than Dan Leno's little 'drawing room music hall' at Walham Green which, in its fifty years of existence, has run the theatrical gamut from the stars of variety and Grand Guignol tragedy to the modern intellectual drama . . . ,[28]

But the Granville closed as a theatre in 1956 and was then used as a television studio. In 1971, Hammersmith Borough Council granted planning permission for it to be replaced by a block of offices and showrooms. Because the theatre was not listed, the case was not referred to the Greater London Council's Historic Buildings Board and by the time the threat to Matcham's faience masterpiece became widely known, it was too late to save it.

The local authority wrongly claimed that it was not possible to impose a building preservation notice and the GLC feared if it served such a notice, the Department of the Environment might decline to endorse it by listing the building, leaving the Council to pay compensation. The Granville was rapidly demolished. John Earl again:

> The sight of that gorgeous auditorium, unroofed and deep in its own debris, will not be forgotten by anyone who saw it. A piece of the magnificent proscenium architrave was taken for the Museum of London. A few pathetic fragments of the deep cream, pale stone, blue-green and warm brown faience scrolls, acanthus ornaments and grotesque marks were picked from the rubble to find homes in private collections, like relics of antiquity. Otherwise, all that remains to remind us of a Matcham invention of rare worth are a few architectural drawings and some inadequate black and white photographs.[29]

As with the Euston Arch, however, some good came out of this loss. The chairman of the GLC's Historic Buildings Board expressed concern that other important buildings by Victorian and Edwardian theatre architects were unprotected and a survey was carried out. Over the following couple of years, 18 more London theatres were listed and the Department of the Environment started to review the listing of theatres throughout Britain. As Earl concluded, 'It is probably not an exaggeration to say that the detailed examination of the national heritage of theatre architecture started in October 1971 as a direct result of the smashing of the Granville'.

With Matcham's theatres, it was the interiors that mattered; with another lost London theatre, it was more the exterior that was of architectural value. The Edwardian Baroque GAIETY THEATRE stood magnificently on the acute corner formed by the junction of the Strand with a new street, the Aldwych. Built in 1902–03, it replaced an earlier Gaiety swept away by the London County Council's Strand Improvement Scheme (a building which began life as the Strand Music Hall designed by the 'rogue' architect, Enoch Bassett Keeling). The architect of the new Gaiety was Ernest Runtz, whose elevations were found unacceptable by the LCC and so Richard Norman Shaw, by now the grand old man of British architecture, was brought in to improve them.

The dome on the curved corner was Runtz's idea, but Shaw proposed the flanking high loggia of paired columns and also improved the design of the higher Gaiety Restaurant behind, which faced the Strand. The Restaurant was not a

▼ The Gaiety Theatre on the corner of the Strand and Aldwych, photographed by Herbert Felton in 1955.

▲▶ The exterior of the Queen's Hall in Langham Place, from a postcard of c.1910 and the interior of the hall photographed by Bedford Lemere in 1894.

success, however, and in 1908 the building became the headquarters of the Marconi Wireless Telegraph Company.

The Gaiety Theatre remained open until the outbreak of the Second World War, during which it was badly damaged by bombing. In 1946, it was bought by Lupino Lane, who attempted to restore the building as a centre for musical comedy but was defeated by the cost as well as building permits and eventually sold at a loss. Then, in 1952, it was acquired by the English Electric Company and, after some controversy, a bland, unimaginative block built on the site by the firm of Adams, Holden & Pearson.

The powerful exterior of the Gaiety, which Pevsner thought, 'Norman Shaw's best design after he had gone classical or Baroque,' was demolished in 1957, although the façade of the Marconi building was permitted to survive.[30] The worthless English Electric building has since been replaced by an hotel designed by Foster & Partners, which at least has a curved tower on the corner but is otherwise scarcely an improvement.

The QUEEN'S HALL in Langham Place was London's pre-eminent concert hall until its destruction in 1941. Renowned for its acoustics, this Late-Victorian building, which opened in 1893, became a centre of excellence for the performance of Classical music. The first manager

was Robert Newman, who founded the Queen's Hall Orchestra and in 1895 began the celebrated Promenade Concerts there, conducted by Henry Wood. F.W.M. Ravenscroft, founder of the Birkbeck Bank, was the promoter of the Queen's Hall and acquired leases for the site just north of Oxford Circus and next to Nash's All Souls' Church in 1885–86. As architect for the proposed concert hall, he chose Thomas Edward Knightley, who happened to be architect to the Birkbeck Bank (see page 84). Construction began in 1891.

Unfortunately, Knightley was accused by the theatre architect C.J. Phipps of using the plan he had prepared for another client interested in building a hall on the same site. The Royal Institute of British Architects adjudicated and found that although the basic plan was indeed Phipps', the elevations and sections and the exterior treatment – a fine design with coupled columns – was Knightley's own unaided effort. The plan, which contributed to the fine acoustic, was rectangular but with a curved end facing the stage. Another positive factor was lining the walls with timber and canvas. The richly decorated main hall originally contained 3,000 seats while the subsidiary Queen's Small Hall could seat 500.

For almost half a century, the Queen's Hall was the focus of London's musical life. Although it suffered bomb damage in 1940, the last performance there was of Elgar's 'The Dream of Gerontius' on 10 May 1941 with the London Philharmonic Orchestra conducted by Malcolm Sargeant. That night, during the heavy raid that also destroyed the House of Commons, the building was completely gutted by an incendiary bomb. After the war, the Queen's Hall was not rebuilt and it was eventually replaced, in 1951, on the other side of the Thames by the Royal Festival Hall which, for all its great merits, has lacked the reputation for acoustic excellence acquired by Knightley's and Phipps' convivial and entertaining building.

Public houses also reached the apotheosis towards the end of Victoria's reign when – as with theatres – there was a building boom. Large numbers of pubs were then rebuilt on a more lavish and yet more respectable scale as the brewers responded to the growing power of the temperance movement. The 1890s was the 'golden age'; as Mark Girouard has written: 'The pubs then were bigger and brighter, their lamps more enormous, their glass more elaborate, their fittings more sumptuous than they had ever been before or were to be again'.[31]

There were certainly many, many more public houses in Victorian Britain than there are today, when the very institution of the pub seems under threat. Victorian pubs as buildings have proved resilient, however, although often no longer in use for their intended purpose. Even in areas subjected to comprehensive development, they have tended to survive (owing to ownership by brewers) on formerly prominent corner sites when all the surrounding housing has been cleared and rebuilt. What has proved vulnerable, however, is their often-sumptuously appointed interiors. Bar fittings, screens and other elaborate woodwork, ornamental mirrors, acid-etched, silvered or gilded glass, decorative tiles and plasterwork and elaborate light fittings – all examples of craftsmanship designed to create a convivial atmosphere and quite as fine as could be found in a contemporary country house – have all too often been mutilated or ripped out by brewers or other owners in a misguided attempt to modernise the drinking establishment or subject it to a fashionable makeover.

Good pub interiors have proved difficult to protect because few pubs have been considered worthy of listing. Although there is now a considerable literature on the history of public houses and historians have succeeded in identifying their usually obscure designers and architects, such buildings have not been taken seriously enough as architecture – whether they are Victorian or earlier, or indeed later in date. As Marcus Binney observed

◀ The interior of the Woodman public house in Birmingham in c.1900.

▶ ▼ The Private Bar and the front of the Woodman pub in Easy Row in Birmingham in c.1900.

in 1983 in a SAVE Britain's Heritage report intended to highlight the continuing threat to fine pub buildings and interiors,

> In the 46 volumes of Sir Nikolaus Pevsner's *Buildings of England* . . . there are a total of 4612 illustrations. Just eight of these are of pubs. Yet pubs are undoubtedly the most visited and most popular of all Britain's historic buildings.[32]

Only a few representative examples of lost Victorian pubs can be included here. One must be a fine example of an 1890s pub in BIRMINGHAM, whose loss is still regretted. The WOODMAN in Easy Row, not far from Birmingham's temple-like Town Hall, was rebuilt in 1891–92 by the obscure local architect Henry Naden. In its latter days it was a favourite of both students and staff from the nearby School of Art, while its predecessor was much frequented by local politicians and even used for Council meetings in the 1850s before the reformist era of Joseph Chamberlain.

Naden's vaguely Early Renaissance style masonry exterior, embellished with a large figure of a woodman, was carried on a single girder so that the whole width of the ground-floor entrance could be an undulating, tantalising screen of glass and timber. Behind this, high quality craftsmanship in timber, glass and tile created a glittering, warm ambience. To quote the historians of Birmingham's pubs, Alan Crawford and Robert Thorne, 'Inside, there was a small Private Bar, its snob-screen and partitions filled with stained glass; the bar-back was sumptuously carved and the walls covered with tiles. In the large Public Bar there were tile pictures of "Old Birmingham"'.[33] All this was destroyed when the buildings in Easy Row were cleared in 1965 to make way for the city's Inner Ring Road.

There was less reason to demolish KEAN'S HOTEL in Park Lane, in LIVERPOOL, which is illustrated here as representative of the hundreds

▲ Kean's Hotel in Park Lane in Liverpool in 1974, shortly before its demolition.

of ebullient, ornamental and cheerful Victorian pub buildings which gave character to the urban scene but have been swept away – usually as a consequence of comprehensive redevelopment. Keen's Hotel was originally the premises of a wine and spirit merchant as well as a public house. Like many such buildings, it was an urban landmark as it stood on a corner higher than the neighbouring terraces of houses.

Each floor was richly ornamented while, above big bold integral lettering, its skyline dissolved into a fantastic composition of pediments, balustrades, urns and finials. Pevsner noticed it: 'a riotous piece, the ground floor juicily decorated, the skyline quite fantastic'.[34] But that didn't stop Kean's Hotel from being swept away in the 1970s, along with all the nearby streets close to the docks and the River Mersey.

4: COMMERCE

The 19th century saw the increasing specialisation and diversification of building types. In the Georgian period, businesses like banks would usually be accommodated in urban buildings little different in appearance to the ordinary domestic terraced house. But Victorian banks and insurance companies wanted to be housed in distinct and distinctive buildings. Elaborate in design, usually Classical but sometimes Gothic, these buildings would be seen as advertisements for the prestige and soundness of the enterprise. New building types also emerged, such as the block of lettable offices and the commercial wholesale warehouse.

Technical developments also influenced the form of commercial architecture. Iron structures allowed the creation of larger banking halls and internal floor spaces, while the new technology of iron and glass was often employed – invariably on the rear, invisible elevation – to bring more light into densely packed urban buildings. Iron and glass was also used behind masonry façades to create the large indoor spaces required in market halls and commercial exchanges. And it was a brilliant combination of civilised Classical architecture and innovative structure that

characterised one of the greatest of lost Victorian commercial buildings. Coming soon after the threat to the Euston Arch, this was a scandalous case which resulted in another defeat for the newly founded Victorian Society and one which has, similarly, not been forgotten or forgiven.

The COAL EXCHANGE in the City of London was really a corporate rather than a commercial structure. Begun in 1846, and opened in 1849 by Prince Albert (who arrived by ceremonial barge on the River Thames), it was designed by James Bunstone Bunning, architect and surveyor to the City Corporation. For Henry-Russell Hitchcock, it was 'the prime City monument of the Early Victorian period' and one in which the architect displayed great accomplishment in creating an internal court which was 'a monument for the ages'.[35]

The exterior of the building, on its corner site, was an elegant and sophisticated Classical composition. Identical palazzo façades faced both St Mary at Hill and Lower Thames Street, while the intervening recessed corner entrance was

◀◀ The Coal Exchange on the corner of St Mary-at-Hill and Lower Thames Street, shortly before demolition began in 1962 (perspective adjusted).

▲▶ The cast-iron rotunda inside the Coal Exchange, photographed by Norman Gold for the Architectural Press in 1958.

defined by a quadrant portico above which rose a circular tower. The interior was dominated by a domed and galleried rotunda 60ft in diameter and 74ft high, which was entirely constructed of cast iron. It was a design both highly functional and expressive, for the iron castings were embellished with a rope motif and the interior further enhanced with painted decoration by Frederick Sang.

With the need for an exchange for coal merchants receding, the Coal Exchange first came under threat in 1956 and two years later the City Corporation announced that Bunning's masterpiece was to be demolished. The ostensible reason was a plan to widen Lower Thames Street by 1972, with the Custom House to the south regarded as immovable, but the potential of the site for redevelopment was also a consideration. The battle for the Coal Exchange waged for four years, with the Victorian Society at first succeeding in the postponement of its destruction. What proved insuperable was the prejudice and lack of imagination of the City Corporation despite the best efforts of the Society (as described earlier) in broadcasting the international significance of the building.

In addition, three schemes were submitted to

the Ministry of Housing and Local Government to show how the road could be widened without destroying the Coal Exchange; that by Lord Mottistone, involving rebuilding the Lower Thames Street front further back and 'arcading' the pavements on both sides of the road, was deemed 'not impracticable' but the Minister nevertheless released the Corporation from its undertaking not to demolish the building.

A last-ditch attempt to raise funds to re-erect the rotunda in Australia was made, but the Corporation was uncooperative and proceeded to demolish the whole building with indecent haste towards the end of 1962. The demolition contractor was Valori: the same firm as took down the Euston Arch.

The Coal Exchange was but one of many fine Victorian buildings in the City of London demolished in the 1960s and 1970s. Another major loss was that of the SUN FIRE OFFICE on the corner of Threadneedle Street, next to the Bank of England. Built, after some complications, in 1841–43, it was designed by the most learned, fastidious and brilliant of 19th-century Classicists, Charles Robert Cockerell. Its architecture drew on the Italian Renaissance as well as the ancient Greek, creating what David Watkin has described as 'that scattered over-all richness of effect, that complex play with flickering wall-planes, that we associate with Italian Mannerism'.[36]

A Greek-Corinthian order united second and third floors below a bracketed cornice, while on the ground floor Cockerell introduced his subsequently influential invention of the haunched segmental arched window. In 1895, the building was cleverly enlarged by the company's architect, F.W. Porter, who inserted an extra storey between first and second floors in a seamless manner. Unfortunately, this change was used as an excuse by the City Corporation to grant permission for demolition in 1969 despite the fact that it was listed and the last surviving building by Cockerell in London. A decade earlier, Goodhart-Rendel had expressed the hope that

> the headquarters of the Westminster Bank, which disappeared from London before the last war, is that last building of Cockerell's that we shall pull down for a very long time. There are not too many of them, and they display a degree of skill in the technique of neo-Classical design that is rare in England.[37]

So it was dismaying that Sir John Summerson argued the 1890s alterations 'so falsified Cockerell's whole intention that demolition could not easily be resisted,' although the architect's biographer disagreed, as did Sir Nikolaus Pevsner, who wrote that the upper floors had been 'actually very well and tactfully altered'.[38] So Cockerell's wonderfully rich and allusive building came down in 1970, to be replaced by an unmemorable new structure for the Royal Bank of Scotland.

In 1861–62, the LONDON AND COUNTY BANK encouraged the aggrandisement of LOMBARD STREET by rebuilding its premises as a handsome palazzo (using Portland stone from old Westminster Bridge). It was designed by C.O. Parnell, best known as the architect of the Whitehall Club, in Whitehall. In 1874–75, the bank was sympathetically extended after Parnell's death by an unknown architect, who treated the corner with Nicholas Lane in a clever manner,

▲ The former Sun Fire Office in Threadneedle Street next to the Bank of England, in 1962.

▲ The former London and County Bank on the south side of Lombard Street, shortly before demolition.

▶ ▼ The Life Association of
Scotland building in Princes
Street in Edinburgh and a
detail of its rich Venetian
Renaissance façade,
photographed in 1963.

setting it back on the diagonal above first floor. Pevsner admired this vigorous essay in 'what might be called a debased palazzo style. Note the big columns on the ground floor with alternating vermiculated rustication'. It was demolished in the mid-1960s, and Pevsner's successor, Simon Bradley, noted in the most recent *Buildings of England* volume for the City of London that its replacement, 'shows what the traffic-obsessed 1960s had in mind for the future of Lombard Street: plain and rectilinear in stone, seven storeys high, set far back for street widening. The long porte-cochère was to facilitate drive-in banking' – an amenity that has never since been required, and Lombard Street was not widened.[39]

As the SAVE Britain's Heritage report, *From Splendour to Banality: The Rebuilding of the City of London 1945–1983*, observed, 'The National Westminster Bank is as soulless and insipid a

replacement as could be imagined.' And that replacement has since been replaced.

Another magnificent Classical commercial building destroyed for no good reason was that erected for the LIFE ASSOCIATION OF SCOTLAND in Princes Street in EDINBURGH, in 1855–58. The great palazzo, which also contained the Bedford Hotel, with a sumptuous, richly modelled façade inspired by Sansovino was designed by David Rhind (with Sir Charles Barry as consultant). The sculpture was by Alexander Handyside Ritchie and originally tall, thin finials rose above the cornice. Henry-Russell Hitchcock considered it, 'the best of all buildings in Britain in the Venetian High Renaissance style'.[40]

In 1954, three architects forming Edinburgh Corporation's Princes Street Panel recommended the city's famous one-sided commercial street be rebuilt with a continuous first-floor walkway. This idiocy was used as an excuse to do away with the two best buildings in the street, which stood side by side close to the Mound and the National Gallery of Scotland: William Burn's New Club of 1834, together with the former head office of the Life Association. A decade later, Rhind's building was threatened with redevelopment. Deplorably, the Cockburn Association did not object, 'provided the subsequent redevelopment is of the highest architectural standard'. As the Victorian Society (then active in Scotland) commented,

As the building is perhaps the best of the few buildings of any merit in the entire length of Princes Street, this decision is a little disappointing. In theory we would agree, but experience has taught us to hold on to what we know to be good until convinced that it will be replaced by something as good or better. So far we have had no cause for such conviction.[41]

The Scottish Georgian Society (today the Architectural Heritage Society of Scotland) and other bodies campaigned against Edinburgh Corporation's acquiescence in the demolition of the building, but the Secretary of State for Scotland declined to intervene – even though it was listed, and it was demonstrated that the walkway could perfectly well be threaded behind the mezzanine storey introduced by Barry. This magnificent commercial palace was demolished in 1967–68. Its replacement, needless to say, merely contributed to the continuing degradation of Princes Street.

The commercial buildings of Victorian GLASGOW were more innovative. Many of these were constructed entirely of cast-iron in the 1850s, incorporating large sheets of plate glass, and Hitchcock, in 1951, considered that, 'Whether their design owes more to architects or to ironfounders, they are among the most successful Victorian commercial edifices to be found on

◀ The Cairney Building on the north side of Bath Street in Glasgow, photographed in 1906 (perspective corrected); its Ionic neighbour is the former Mechanics Institute by James Salmon, since altered.

▶ The Royal Exchange in
Middlesbrough in 1981.

either side of the Atlantic'.[42] All but two have since been destroyed.

The most truly original and innovative commercial buildings in the city in which masonry and metal construction was combined were those designed by Alexander 'Greek' Thomson in his personal Modern Greek style. Perhaps the most remarkable was the CAIRNEY BUILDING in Bath Street. Built in 1860–61 for John Cairney, stained-glass manufacturer, the design of its powerfully modelled façade played with ambiguities in wall planes and structural supports. Large plate-glass windows were at ground level, while at the top Thomson introduced his idea of an 'eaves gallery', where the fenestration was a screen of timber and glass entirely separate from his colonnade of exotic square piers – a device he would use again. The roof above the cornice contained a sloping skylight.

Hitchcock considered this building, 'one of the finest of all Victorian warehouses'[43] but it disappeared to make way for an extension of the Corporation's Transport Offices in about 1935 – that is, three decades before the great municipal holocaust of Victorian Glasgow.

MIDDLESBROUGH, largely a Victorian creation, was similarly ravaged in the 20th century. Here, the ROYAL EXCHANGE was one of a handful of buildings that gave dignity and interest to the centre of the bleak industrial town. Designed by Charles J. Adams and built in 1866–68, it had powerful elevations in red brick which were somehow reminiscent of the work of Vanbrugh – an association more clear when splendid chimneys rose from the corner pavilion. Redundant and neglected, the Exchange was demolished in 1985 to make way for a flyover on the destructive new road, which almost did for the nearby Bell Brothers' Offices by Philip Webb.

In LIVERPOOL, the EXCHANGE was behind the Town Hall. The first Exchange, a Greek Revival building of 1803–08, was replaced in 1864–67 by buildings enclosing three sides of Exchange Flags. These were designed in a rich French Renaissance manner by a member of the Wyatt dynasty of architects, Thomas Henry Wyatt, and had fine rusticated arcades at ground level. But these buildings were systematically demolished from the late 1930s onwards to be replaced by the present Exchange Buildings by Gunton & Gunton – higher, and perhaps purer stylistically, but otherwise scarcely an improvement.

Many distinctive and solidly built commercial

buildings in BRADFORD perished in the comprehensive redevelopment mania of the 1960s. Their stonework may have been blackened by industrial pollution, but underneath they were solidly built. Far too often, a superficial perception of griminess permitted gratuitous destruction. One particularly sad loss was that of the SWAN ARCADE. A large block designed by Milnes & France in the Italianate style and built in 1877–81, it had six grand entrances and contained four linked shopping arcades, with glazed iron roofs as well as much other commercial accommodation. Although – or because – it was a going concern, right in the heart of Bradford and much loved, it was bought by the Arndale Property Trust and razed in 1962. Christopher Hammond has written that,

> the demolition of the Swan Arcade stands in relation to Bradford in the same way that the demolition of Pennsylvania Station stands in relation to New York: the realisation that development plans, mooted with such self assurance and with such financial clout, can lead, without the real apprehension of ordinary citizens, to the irreversible destruction of familiar landmark buildings.[44]

▼ The central arcade in Bradford's Swan Arcade building in c.1960, looking towards the Wool Exchange in Market Street

▶ The central arcade in the
Swan Arcade building being
demolished in 1962.

▼ The arcaded façade of
Kassapian's Warehouse
in Leeds Road in front of
Bradford Exchange Station
in 1943.

At least the loss of the Swan Arcade was so regretted that when the same developers proposed the demolition of the Wool Exchange on the opposite side of Market Street, the fine Gothic Revival building was bought by Bradford City Council to avert the same fate.

Eli Milnes of the firm of Milnes & France designed many of the substantial wool warehouses once such a feature of the city. Derek Lindstrum wrote how, 'it was in Bradford that the "home-trade" warehouse, in which was stocked a wide range of textiles to display to buyers, was raised to a level of architectural magnificence which caused them to be described justifiably as "palatial structures the most splendid of their kind in the kingdom".[45]

Several of these survive in the area known as Little Germany, but some of the best, which stood in LEEDS ROAD and Peel Square, have gone. A fine group dating from *c.* 1860, which stood in front of Exchange Station – all built of stone in Milnes' own rugged version of the arcaded Italianate manner – were entirely swept away in the 1960s. One, lately the warehouse of KASSAPIAN Sons Ltd, 'academically Roman', was noticed, illustrated and praised by Henry-Russell Hitchcock as one of 'two masterpieces of the genre at its best moment'.[46]

In nearby LEEDS, the finest commercial street was Park Row, which Pevsner thought, 'gave the full flavour of commercial Leeds'.[47] Almost every one of the fine buildings by Alfred Waterhouse, George Corson and others – all depicted in an evocative painting of Park Row by Atkinson Grimshaw – disappeared in the 1960s as the street was almost systematically redeveloped. Perhaps the greatest loss was BECKETT'S BANK, whose modern Gothic elevations were designed in brick and stone by George Gilbert Scott for the family business of that rebarbative architectural amateur and meddler, Edmund Beckett Denison, later Sir Edmund Beckett and later still Lord Grimthorpe. Constructed in 1863–67, the building lasted for exactly a century, being demolished in 1964.

▲▶ The interior of the galleried hall and the open court of the Columbia Market, photographed in 1915.

One extraordinary Gothic Revival building is best discussed here although it is difficult to categorise and was, in fact, a resounding commercial failure. The COLUMBIA MARKET in the East End of London was described by Pevsner as, 'easily the most spectacular piece of design in Bethnal Green and one of the great follies of the Victorian Age.' It was built in 1864–69 by Baroness Burdett-Coutts, pious Evangelical heiress and generous philanthropist, on a notorious slum site originally suggested to her by Charles Dickens, who was also interested in social reform. Angela Burdett-Coutts' aim was to provide an open market with fair prices for East Enders, who were excluded from traditional markets like Billingsgate and were victims of other monopolies and traders.

Her architect was Henry Darbishire, who had earlier designed for her the grim minimally Gothic blocks of social housing erected around Columbia Square next door and later became architect to the Peabody Trust. But for the high, noble purpose of the market, dedicated to honest trading, a richer, more correct Gothic was considered appropriate. Market buildings of brick and stone with open arcades were arranged around an open court (later covered with an iron and glass roof). At one end was a tall, galleried hall, 'a structure as proud as any Flemish Guildhall of the prosperous Late Middle Ages', with large gabled Decorated windows and a central tower. Inside, timber vaults were carried on thin clustered columns. Pious texts carved into the stonework reflected the Christian idealism of the foundress.

The Columbia Market cost Burdett-Coutts some £200,000 and was an immediate failure: the vested interests and monopolies prevented wholesalers from supplying it; few shops moved in and within six months, she was forced to hand it over to the City of London. Having attempted to run it as a fish market, the City handed it back in 1874. Three years later, it re-opened as a market for American meat. Soon after, it was reported that, 'Scarcely any of the shops which open upon the arcades are occupied; indeed, very little in the way of business is ever carried on there'.[48] The whole enterprise was finally closed in 1885; most of the buildings then stood empty, though for a time the Great Hall used as the headquarters of the East London Church Polytechnic.

In 1915, the complex was purchased by the London County Council, which used it for storage. Pevsner, in 1952, considered that, 'the building should be preserved at all cost and made some reasonable use of.'[49] Others disagreed. In his lecture on 'Victorian Conservanda' which attempted to suggest by what criteria the newly founded Victorian Society should decide what buildings were worth fighting for, Goodhart-Rendel recalled John Summerson had said that he would see no harm in the destruction of the market and,

> I think in saying so he was quite right. To stand in the deserted nave of that extraordinary structure and to reflect upon the magnificent but unrealistic philanthropy of its founder is certainly to intensify one's perception of a lost Victorian attitude of mind. It also may be to raise one's wonder that a lady of great wealth, enjoying the especial confidence and applause of her monarch, should have entrusted the realisation of her noble dream to a practically unknown architect, who seems to have been incapable of producing a decent building of any kind.[50]

Both market and tenements were demolished between 1958 and 1966, to be replaced by blocks of flats as grim in their way as Darbishire's. Unlike, say, the Kirkgate Market in Bradford, the project was a failure, unpopular and useless, but it is still difficult not to lament the loss of such a magnificent Gothic white elephant.

Gothic was used for many Victorian commercial buildings. One such was the centrepiece of a Victorian commercial district, which was the subject of one of the greatest conservation battles of the late-20th century. MANSION HOUSE BUILDINGS or No.1 Poultry was a prominent and much-loved landmark in the City of London, close to the Mansion House and the Bank of England. Designed by the family firm of Belcher & Belcher, the junior partner being John Belcher, the future architect of the Institute of Chartered Accountants, this block of offices and shops was built in 1870–71.

One shop became the premises of the jewellers Mappin & Webb, situated on the curved corner between Queen Victoria Street and Poultry, which was marked by a circular conical-roofed turret. Queen Victoria Street had been cut through from the Victoria Embankment in 1867–71 and almost

▶ The threatened wedge-shaped group of mid-Victorian commercial buildings between Queen Victoria Street and Poultry photographed in c.1984 by the author from in front of the Mansion House.

all of the buildings on the site bounded by this street, Poultry and the intervening ancient lane, Bucklersbury, dated from the 1870s and formed a diverse and eclectic mix.

A century later, all these, plus the Victorian triangular block on the south side, were to be

▼ The varied group of buildings along Poultry threatened with redevelopment.

swept away to create Mansion House Square, a gratuitous and alien rectangular space intended as a setting for an 18-storey tower on the west side designed by the German-American modernist Mies van der Rohe. Conceived in the 1960s by Peter Palumbo, the son of the notorious property developer Rudolph Palumbo, it was not until the early 1980s that the necessary leases were acquired for the scheme. By then not only was van der Rohe dead and the concept dated, but popular opposition to the wholesale redevelopment of historic areas and the sort of rich, small-scaled urban streetscape represented by the Poultry site had grown. No one building on the site was of the highest architectural quality but it was now recognised that, together, they had 'group value'.

A momentous public inquiry into the project was held in 1984. The following year, after a long interval of what was assumed to be political wrangling, the (Conservative) Secretary of State endorsed the Inspector's decision to reject the Mies tower. This seemed to be a defeat for the Modernist establishment and a victory for the conservation cause but a gratuitous, partisan rider by the Secretary of State, Patrick Jenkin, encouraged Palumbo to try again with 'an acceptable scheme'.[51] James Stirling was then commissioned to redevelop just the triangular site and his scheme again opposed by the Victorian Society, SAVE Britain's Heritage, the Greater London Council, English Heritage and others.

A second public enquiry was held in 1988. In this case, the Secretary of State did not have to worry about overruling his Inspector, as the latter, after a long interval, allowed the demolition of eight listed buildings and approved the Stirling design, observing that 'might just be a masterpiece'. This decision undermined the presumption in favour of the retention of listed buildings and it was successfully challenged by SAVE Britain's Heritage in the Court of Appeal but finally confirmed in the House of Lords. All the buildings on the site were cleared in 1994. Whether the replacement block designed by James Stirling, Michael Wilford & Associates in a gimmicky Post-Modern manner is in fact a masterpiece must remain a matter of opinion.

Most Victorian buildings in the City of London were more or less Classical while a few – like No. 1 Poultry – were Gothic. What was more unusual, and revolutionary in its way, was the block of lettable offices built in Leadenhall Street, in 1871–73. NEW ZEALAND CHAMBERS was also the premises of the shipping line, Shaw Savill & Co., and one of the partners turned to his brother, the up-and-coming domestic architect Richard Norman Shaw, for the design.

For this commercial building, Shaw used the new 'Queen Anne' style he was developing for his town houses. Between tall brick piers, he placed tiers of delicate timber oriel windows while an artful asymmetry was introduced on the ground floor. Shaw's biographer, Andrew Saint, observes that the design was inspired by the house then standing in Bishopsgate in which the Elizabethan merchant, Sir Paul Pindar, had lived, so the imagery was mercantile as well as vernacular; the oriel windows also let in plenty of light. The design caused a great stir and older architects were shocked. Professor Donaldson wondered what could have induced Shaw 'to rake up a type of the very lowest state of corrupt erection in the City of London, of a period that marks the senility of decaying taste'.[52] But for younger architects the building pointed a way forwards; as John Summerson concluded:

▲ New Zealand Chambers in Leadenhall Street, photographed in 1931.

from the moment of building New Zealand Chambers, Shaw took the lead in English architecture – the lead so long and so firmly held by Sir Charles Barry.

What is more, the offices let quickly and at high rents. But the large areas of timber and glass were highly vulnerable to incendiary bombs in the raids of 1940 and 1941 and, as Summerson recalled, the building,

burned almost to the ground – not quite, however, and the beautifully modelled doorway and *oeil-de-boeuf* window in brick remained for many years in pleasing isolation.[53]

Norman Shaw's other building in the City of London perished at the hands of the City Corporation rather than by enemy bombs. In 1880–81, he rebuilt the front of the premises of BARINGS BANK in Bishopsgate. By now, Shaw was moving from the picturesque characteristic of his earlier work towards a more sober and correct Classicism and he gave Barings the appearance of a gentlemanly red brick mansion in the true style of the reign of Queen Anne. In 1913 a northern extension in a similar style was added by his

▶ Barings Bank and the Banque Belge on the east side of Bishopsgate in 1968 six years before they were cleared; in the distance is Gibson's National Provincial Bankfor whose retention the Victorian Society campaigned successfully.

▼ The former Birkbeck Penny Bank in Southampton Buildings behind Holborn in 1965.

pupil Gerald Horsley; the interior was later partly reconstructed by Lutyens.

In the 1960s it was decided that the east side of Bishopsgate must be widened because of the rebuilding of London Bridge. This required the demolition of Barings Bank, along with the neighbouring Banque Belge, with its fine stone front of the 1920s by Edwin Cooper. The Victorian Society fought long and hard against this, but the buildings were cleared in 1974. Today, their overweening replacements stand back from the road behind trees, for, as Gracechurch Street further south was, in the event, allowed to remain narrow, the road widening was entirely pointless. Barings Bank was sacrificed in vain.

One of the most magnificent of all Late-Victorian commercial buildings was the former BIRKBECK PENNY BANK on the south side of High Holborn, near Chancery Lane. Pevsner called it, 'a phantasmagoria in majolica' as it was faced in ceramic, inside and out. It was designed by the bank's house architect, T.E. Knightley, also the architect of the Queen's Hall (see page 66), and built in 1895–1902. On the exterior were coupled peacock-green columns and portrait medallions of such worthies as Michelangelo, Flaxman, Brunel, Tennyson and Pugin; inside was a huge domed and galleried banking hall, 72ft in diameter (that is, larger than Soane's Rotunda in the Bank of England) decorated with

◀ ▾ The magnificent ceramic banking hall of the former Birkbeck Penny Bank, photographed in 1965.

▶ McGeogh's Warehouse on the corner of Cadogan and West Campbell Streets in Glasgow photographed in 1969, shortly before its demolition.

Doulton's Carrara ware, glazed tiles and murals. 'The whole chamber glitters with a glory of freshly washed glazed tiling in a colour scheme of cream buff and brown,' wrote an architect visitor in 1948:

> with a sparing use of sage green on the lower pilasters and golden mosaic in the dome. Arabesques, diaper patterns and fantastic dragon brackets alike look as fresh as they must have done on the day they were made . . .[54]

The Birkbeck Bank folded a decade after this majolica palace opened and the building was taken over by the Westminster Bank. In 1964, the Victorian Society learned that planning permission had already been granted for its demolition, so revoking it would have required the local authority to compensate its owners. An appeal to the Westminster Bank was unavailing. The bank closed the following year and the wonderful majolica was smashed to make way for

what is now the former National Westminster House, a banal 1960s eight-storey block, which lurches along High Holborn. Had Knightley's amazing creation survived, it would, of course, have made a splendid restaurant now that the branch bank has become a thing of the past.

The last lost commercial building illustrated here stood in Glasgow rather than London and dated from the reign of Edward VII. McGEOGH'S WAREHOUSE was designed by the third of the great architects of international stature to emerge from the city: John James Burnet. William McGeogh's ironmongery warehouse was built in 1905–10 and, like the contemporary work of C.R. Mackintosh, represented a brilliant fusion of tradition and modernity. The vertical piers on its free Baroque-style stone exterior, enriched with sculpture, reflected the internal steel structure, and may well have been influenced by the work of Louis Sullivan in North America, with which Burnet was familiar, although they were also a development of ideas explored by 'Greek' Thomson. It was also one of the earliest buildings to use reinforced concrete slabs cast in situ. 'Here,' wrote the historians of Glasgow's architecture, Andor Gomme and David Walker:

> the interest in the vertical articulation of the façade achieves its triumph, and provides a near perfect expression of the constructional techniques which Burnet was likewise pioneering . . . McGeogh's is the high-water mark of Burnet in Glasgow: of its type the city has nothing finer.[55]

So, in the orgy of self-destruction which consumed Glasgow in the 1960s and 1970s, it was proposed for demolition. Glasgow City Council at first placed a Preservation Order on the building but, despite the urging of the Victorian Society, the Secretary of State for Scotland declined to confirm this. The Council then decided not to object to demolition. This extraordinary building came down in 1970. As similarly threatened buildings by Mackintosh managed to survive, its loss has gravely distorted our understanding of the architectural history of Glasgow and of the early 20th century in Britain.

5: INDUSTRIAL

Some of the most impressive and representative structures erected during the 19th century were industrial buildings, whether factories, mills, storage warehouses or dock buildings. Many, in their gaunt sublimity, continued the 'Functional Tradition' of Georgian industrial architecture, relying on good proportions and repetition to give interest to multi-storey structures of brick or stone. But, towards the end of the century, industrial architecture tended to become more elaborate, with some buildings enlivened by decorative terra-cotta or other forms of ornament, while some tall factory chimneys might be made to look vaguely like Giotto's Tower in Florence, or another famous Italian campanile.

Industrial buildings have also proved to be some of the most problematic and vulnerable of Victorian buildings. With the decline of the traditional industries of the North of England and Scotland after the 1920s and the Depression, many mills and warehouses were redundant, while since the Second World War almost all Northern cities became ashamed of their Victorian industrial legacy. Seeing this as dark, dirty and oppressive, they became rather over-anxious to replace it by something new and presumed better. In the 1960s,

film of the demolition of the tall chimneys that once characterised the urban skyline of so much of Britain was regularly broadcast on television. In some cities, like Glasgow, all tangible evidence of the industrial past that made the city great and prosperous would seem to have been almost systematically expunged.

Comparatively few of the lost Victorian industrial buildings may be regarded as of architectural importance, and only a few representative examples can be included here. But almost all were evocative and substantial structures which were not only of historical importance, whether local or national, but perfectly capable of gainful re-use – as the successful adaptation of such buildings as the Albert Dock in Liverpool, Titus Salt's mill at Saltaire and Dean Clough Mills at Halifax have demonstrated. A huge number of fine industrial buildings were destroyed before attitudes changed. As Kenneth Powell wrote for the pioneering 'Satanic Mills' exhibition organised by SAVE Britain's Heritage in 1979:

◀◀ Coldhurst Mill in Oldham, Lancashire, photographed by Randolph Langenbach days before its demolition.

▶ St Mary Overy's Wharf in Southwark, close to London Bridge, photographed by Robert Carr in 1979.

It is still widely believed conservation and economic growth are incompatible, that conservation implies no change. In the textile producing towns of northern England physical decay and destruction have gone hand in hand with economic decline. Yet to squander the achievements of the greatest age in our history seems sheer folly.[56]

What happened in OLDHAM in Lancashire was all too typical. Oldham was the site of the greatest concentration of textile mills in Britain, and possibly in the world. At the height of its prosperity there were well over 200 mills and 19 million of Britain's 50 million spindles were in Oldham. Most of the mills were built in the 1870s and they were remarkably similar in the use of the Romanesque style or a French Second Empire manner – partly because many were designed by the same local practice founded by A.H. Stott and continued by his sons. Decline and depression came in the 1930s and up to the 1970s the mills and their chimneys dominated.

It was the wrong image, so, in 1977, Oldham District Council sought an Act of Parliament to enable mills to be declared 'unfit' for almost any reason and then demolished, in the naïve belief that new industry would automatically spring up in

their place. The estates officer was quoted as believing that, 'the mills are unsightly and deny the use of a site to more modern premises'. But cleared sites proved even more unsightly. As the American photographer Randolph Langenbach asked, 'What purpose can be served by a wholesale demolition of the mills? How can an improvement of the Oldham environment be accomplished by demolishing the most substantial buildings within it?'[57]

COLDHURST MILL was built in 1876 and was photographed just over a century later by Mr Langenbach in his survey of Oldham; a week later it had disappeared.

The part of Southwark immediately over London Bridge is the oldest inhabited area of the South Bank of the Thames. Here stood the Mediaeval town residence of the Bishop of Winchester and the Priory of St Mary Overie, whose church is now Southwark Cathedral. Close by was ST MARY OVERY'S WHARF, reflecting the later commercial and industrial history of this part of the capital. The Victorian building on the site was constructed in 1882–83 and designed by George A. Dunnage. Inside, the floors were supported on cast-iron columns. The exterior was all of brick. Towards the river and facing the wharf inlet, the brickwork was in two colours and ornamental, with gables placed above the vertically-stacked loading bays. At the rear, towards Clink Street, the architecture was simpler, with a tall, blank curved brick corner containing a staircase treated in the best sublime manner of the Functional Tradition.

Clink Street and the surrounding streets formed one of the most atmospheric industrial urban landscapes in the capital and was declared a conservation area by the London Borough of Southwark. St Mary Overy's Wharf was listed, at Grade II. As part of the process which has led to the transformation of this once derelict area, European Ferries applied to replace the wharf building with a new office block. This was opposed by Southwark, by the Greater London Council and by the Victorian Society, who argued that, despite damage caused by two fires, the seven-storey structure was essentially sound and the building capable of refurbishment for a new purpose.

A public inquiry was held in 1981. The following year, the Inspector recommended against demolition but this judgement was overruled by the Secretary of State for the Environment, Michael Heseltine. In 1984, because the redevelopment plans had changed and the proposal to dock Captain Scott's ship *HMS Discovery* in the wharf abandoned, the MP for Southwark, Simon Hughes, appealed in Parliament for the retention of St Mary Overy's Wharf.

▲ The dramatic rear of St Mary Overy's Wharf photographed by the author in 1982.

> The building has been there for 100 years. It is part of a particularly historic part of our city. It would be nothing less than a tragedy if, unnecessarily, it were now pulled down. The Secretary of State is the only person with the power to stop its demolition and so enhance the conservation of our heritage along the Thames. I beseech the Secretary of State, on behalf of thousands of people, of our city and of the nation, to think again.

But the Secretary of State chose not to do so. This magnificent industrial building was destroyed and, to add insult to injury, a pathetic bogus replica of Francis Drake's *Golden Hinde* placed in the wharf.

Much more elaborate was the factory by the Thames, further upstream on the South Bank, for it was built as a living advertisement for its products. DOULTON & CO.'S POTTERY was first established in Lambeth, in 1815. Under Henry Doulton in the 1870s, the firm began to produce more decorative ceramics, many designed by talented designers from the nearby Lambeth School of Art, notably George Tinworth. In 1876–77, prominent new buildings were erected on the Albert Embankment. These were elaborate, rumbustuous exercises in Ruskinian Gothic, highly ornamented with terra-cotta detail from the Doulton factory, and designed by J. Stark Wilkinson and F.W. Tarring in collaboration with Doulton's usual architects, Waring & Nicholson.

The factory chimney behind, 233ft high, was inspired by the campanile of the Palazzo Vecchio in Florence. From these buildings and others built later nearby came the Lambeth faience, Carrara Ware and the other colourful ceramic products that ornamented so many Late-Victorian and

▶ Doulton & Co.'s Pottery on the Albert Embankment in Lambeth in 1940.

Edwardian buildings, like the Birkbeck Bank and the Granville Theatre (see above).

In 1935–39 an office block for Doulton's was erected further north on the Albert Embankment, as dull as the other 20th-century buildings, which made this stretch of riverside so uninviting. The Victorian buildings were gutted during the Second World War and demolished between 1952 and 1958 (the 1930s block went in 1978). Royal Doulton transferred all production to Stoke-on-Trent in 1956, partly because the Clean Air Act prevented the production of salt glaze ware. However, a separate Gothic block, built in 1878 inland on the corner of Lambeth High Street and Black Prince Road, survives

◀ One of the corner turrets on J.& P. Coats' No.1 Spinning Mill at Paisley in 1992.

to show how splendid and enlivening the Albert Embankment buildings must have been.

One of the most splendid and impressive of all Victorian factories was in PAISLEY in Scotland. James Coats established his cotton thread-spinning business in 1802 and Victorian Paisley was dominated by two families in this trade: Coats and Clark. By the end of the century, after the two businesses had amalgamated, some 10,000 people were employed in the Clarks' Anchor Mills and the Coats' Ferguslie Mills. Both families paid for most of the public buildings that ornament the ancient town of Paisley for the benefit of its citizens, such as the Clark Town Hall and the Coats Observatory and the Coats Memorial Church.

In 1887, Messrs J. & P. Coats built the NO.1 SPINNING MILL on their FERGUSLIE site, a vast, fireproof structure of cast-iron and reinforced concrete, which housed all the mechanised processes involved in spinning yarn from raw cotton. Designed by Woodhouse & Morley, architects, of Bradford, its repetitively fenestrated walls were built of red brick and stone and topped with a bracketed cornice and a balustrade; domed turrets were placed above each corner. The Spinning Mill was a visible symbol of the importance and prestige of the Coats enterprise. But with the decline of the thread

The magnificent derelict No.1 Spinning Mill at Ferguslie in Paisley photographed in 1992 by the author shortly before the demolition of this listed building was permitted.

industry in the mid-20th century, the Ferguslie site was eventually abandoned.

Splendid and solid, the Spinning Mill could have been converted into flats or used to house small businesses – the useful fate eventually found for the Anchor Mills. But, consumed by self-hatred and uninterested in the positive lessons offered by converted mill buildings in Saltaire and Halifax, Renfrew District Council was determined to wipe out what it regarded as the shameful relics of Paisley's capitalist past and repeatedly tried to raze

the building. As it was listed at the highest grade – category 'A' – this could only be done with the permission of the Secretary of State for Scotland who, shamefully, finally acquiesced in 1992. The great Spinning Mill was cleared – although some smaller ancillary structures, such as the gatehouses and the Counting House, were spared. A housing estate, mediocre and characterless in design, was built on the site, yet there was no reason why new housing could not have been combined with the Spinning Mill converted into flats.

6: PLACES OF WORSHIP

Churches inevitably loom large in any survey of 19th-century architecture. The Victorian Age was a great age of faith and saw the building of a huge number of churches. As every denomination wanted its own place of worship, church buildings proliferated in cities. In London, church building reached a peak in the 1870s when, on average, 11 new churches were opened every year and many of these were of considerable ambition and quality. In the mid-Victorian decades, church architecture was in the vanguard and many of the finest and most representative examples of Victorian architecture are places of worship. This was because of the integral connection between style and faith established by the great Pugin, who argued compellingly that Gothic was the only true Christian style.

Although he was a Roman Catholic convert, Pugin's writings had the most immediate influence on Anglican church architects, although the predilection for Gothic eventually affected every denomination. The vigorous crusade for Gothic combined with the revitalisation of the Church of England after the 1840s meant that ambitious young architects were most eager to build churches in the 1840s, 1850s and 1860s. Many innovations which invigorated the Gothic Revival, such as using structural polychromy and following Continental precedents, were first tried in church buildings and many of the leading mid-Victorian architects – Scott, Street, Butterfield, Bodley, Pearson – were primarily ecclesiastical designers. Even at the end of the century church architecture retained its prestige.

Many of the finest lost Victorian buildings are, therefore, religious buildings. Some were victims of war, some of population movements and urban redevelopments, which led to their redundancy, but most have gone because of the general decline in church attendance in the 20th century. Faced with falling congregations and rising maintenance costs, not just the Church of England but all denominations found that many of their buildings were too large or surplus to requirements. In 1980, SAVE Britain's Heritage found that chapels had formed the largest category of notable buildings in danger with which the campaigning body had been concerned. As Marcus Binney wrote at the time:

◀◀ "No modern church is finer": Holy Trinity Church, Bingley, in Yorkshire seen from the south-east in 1973; the school in the foreground was of recent date.

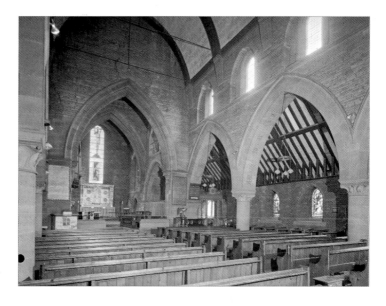

▶ The interior of Holy Trinity, Bingley, looking east, photographed by Gordon Barnes in 1968.

The nonconformist contribution to British architecture has been calamitously underestimated. On the one hand establishment architectural historians have written the history of English architectural history solely in terms of the parish church and the cathedral. On the other hand, the nonconformists themselves have shown little interest in the numerous ambitious and often delightful or inspiring buildings they have erected.[58]

Of the many churches and chapels chosen for closure, some were converted to new uses. This often proved easier with nonconformist chapels, with their wide interior spaces unencumbered by arcades, while the adaptation of typical Anglican churches, with their separate aisles and chancels, has all too often been severely detrimental to their architectural quality and interest. But far too many churches have simply been demolished or abandoned, often after suffering neglect and vandalism, which could, and should, have been avoided.

The situation was exacerbated by the 'ecclesiastical exemption' from normal planning control for churches in use, against which the Victorian Society campaigned from the beginning.

'Churches and church buildings, like railway stations and railway buildings, are outside the law,' the Society complained in 1965. Furthermore, in the Church of England, the Pastoral Measure of 1969 allowed for the alternative use of, or the demolition of churches deemed redundant. This measure allowed for a 'waiting period' to seek a new use for the building, during which it was all too often subject to theft and severe vandalism, leaving demolition as the only realistic option. In the Roman Catholic Church and the nonconformist churches, in which decisions made by individual congregations were paramount (as with synagogues), there was little internal control over the demolition or mutilation of fine buildings.

A few good Victorian churches perished before the Second World War, but most casualties occurred in the first two decades of the Victorian Society's existence, when some of the finest Victorian and Edwardian churches – and, therefore, some of the very best examples of Victorian architecture – were demolished, sometimes after shameful, culpable neglect. In one of the very worst cases, however, a great church disappeared with a bang, rather than after a period of redundancy and decay.

HOLY TRINITY CHURCH, BINGLEY, in

Yorkshire, was an early work by Richard Norman Shaw. As far as Goodhart-Rendel was concerned, 'No modern church is finer'.[59] It was an essay in tough, austere High Victorian Gothic, built in 1866–68, but enlivened with superb stained glass by William Morris' firm. The most conspicuous feature, a tremendous crossing tower surmounted by a pyramidal spire, was added later, in 1880–81, after a redesign. Unfortunately, this proved too ambitious and the weight of the tower soon caused problems. In 1973, cracks in the tower were found to be widening and some feared imminent collapse. The church was closed and the adjacent school evacuated.

The Victorian Society pressed for a proper structural survey to be made of the steeple to see if it could be stabilised, but the vicar and half the congregation wanted to be rid of their Victorian building; the propinquity of the school too added an exaggerated urgency to the situation. It was agreed that part of the spire be taken down to lessen the load, but after a partial collapse during this work the authorities decided to dynamite the whole building. This took place on 7 April 1974 (see page 26). Shaw's biographer, Andrew Saint, comments that this was, 'among the consummate, most assured church interiors of the High Victorian movement; its destruction was an inestimable loss'[60] – which could have been averted. Other fine Victorian churches also disappeared with the help of high explosives, but at least they were the victims of enemy action rather than of the myopic decisions of their owners and guardians.

HOLY TRINITY CHURCH, BESSBOROUGH GARDENS, Westminster, with its tall spire over the crossing was a prominent landmark close to Vauxhall Bridge. Designed by John Loughborough Pearson, the future architect of Truro Cathedral, and built in 1849–52, it was a fine example of a 'correct' Gothic church inspired by Pugin and was much admired when it was completed – not least by Pugin himself. The *Ecclesiologist*, the architectural organ of the Anglican High Church party, opined that, 'When in this church we behold the ideas for which we have fought and suffered obloquy so prominently exhibited, we can indeed thankfully and sincerely offer our Deo

⏶ Holy Trinity Church, Bessborough Gardens, Westminster, photographed by John Summerson in the 1930s.

Gratias'.[61] The church was burned out during the Second World War, but could have been repaired; the site was cleared instead in the mid-1950s.

ST ALKMUND'S CHURCH in DERBY was a Mediaeval church standing in a Georgian square which was rebuilt in 1846 by Henry Isaac Stevens. The new building was an accomplished Gothic design, with a 216ft tall spire, rising above the crossing tower. Many felt that this was an Anglican riposte to the prominent new Roman Catholic nearby church by Pugin (which never received its intended spire above the tall west tower), which had been built a little further north from the city centre, just a few years earlier. Some 20ft of the top of St Alkmund's spire was removed in the 1950s because of structural problems. Then, a decade later, in 1967–68, the whole church was removed to make way for Derby's disastrous inner ring road, which at least spared Pugin's St Mary's, although it was left teetering on the edge of a deep cutting.

▲▶ A distant view along Bridgegate of the exterior of St Alkmund's Church in Derby in 1966 after the removal of the top of its spire (the tower of Pugin's St Marie's is also visible) and the interior photographed by G.B. Mason in 1942.

▼ St Augustine's R.C. Church in Tunbridge Wells in 1967.

ST AUGUSTINE'S, TUNBRIDGE WELLS, was an early and elegant Roman Catholic church designed in 1838 by Joseph Ireland. The flanking campanile was added in 1889 by Brett A. Elphick. In 1966, the church was sold with the intention of building a larger, new place of worship elsewhere in the town and the borough council gave planning permission for a Tesco supermarket to be built on the site. St Augustine's was listed and the Victorian Society argued that the sale and rebuilding proposal was a misuse of the 'ecclesiastical exemption' and that once the church ceased to be used, normal listed building controls should intervene. However, as detailed planning permission for the supermarket had already been granted by the compliant local authority, compensation would be prohibitive if the listed building was retained. The church was therefore demolished. The Society also argued that, if the congregation had to move, it could occupy Christ Church Tunbridge Wells, a nearby Anglican church. In the event, a new St Augustine's was built in 1974–75 and Christ Church, a lumpish

Pugin's Jesus Chapel next to Ackworth Grange in Yorkshire, and its derelict interior with an Easter sepulchre, photographed by G.B. Mason in 1958.

Neo-Norman building, was rebuilt in 1996. Tunbridge Wells has not gained thereby.

St Augustine's Tunbridge Wells was not the sort of Roman Catholic building Welby Pugin cared for, being in a 'Pagan' rather than a Christian style. His Gothic ideal was beautifully expressed in a small private chapel built for an old Catholic family in the West Riding of Yorkshire. The JESUS CHAPEL at ACKWORTH GRANGE near Pontefract was built in 1841–42 for Mrs Elizabeth Tempest, for her family and the local Catholic community. The Gothic chapel, with separate nave and chancel and a chantry chapel with a family vault, was built, somewhat incongruously, alongside a twin bow-fronted Late-Georgian house. It was richly appointed and ornamented, with stained glass, sculpture, a Rood screen and Minton tiles on the floor.

Pugin, who called it the 'Church of the Sacred Heart of Jesus near Pomfret', described it as 'a very faithful revival of a small religious edifice of the fine period of Edward the Third'.[62] A century later it was abandoned, after a second Catholic church had been established in High Ackworth in 1920 and a new church built in 1939. When Pevsner saw Pugin's exquisite creation in the late 1950s, it was 'disused, the movable furnishings have unfortunately been taken away, and the stained glass designed by Pugin is partly broken'.[63] Such was local piety. The chapel was finally demolished in 1966.

Another lost work by Pugin was in a city rather than in the country. ST MARY'S CHURCH in LIVERPOOL was built for that city's rapidly increasing Roman Catholic population in 1843–45. His modern biographer describes it as 'one of the greatest losses to Pugin's oeuvre, for it sounded themes that were to recur in the debates on urban church architecture later in the century'.[64]

The church was first built on a confined site in Edmund Street, with only the east and west elevations having a street frontage. Inside, it was long and narrow, with most light coming from a high clerestory; the nave was tall, flanked by low aisles and with no chancel arch. In the mid-1880s this building was taken down, along with the surrounding houses, to make way for the widening of Exchange Station. In 1885, it was carefully rebuilt by the architect's eighth and last child – Peter Paul Pugin – on a new site further west in Highfield Street. This was more open, with an exposed south wall, and the church now acquired a south porch surmounted by a monstrous pinnacle. St Mary's was bombed in 1941 and a fine new church built on the site. This too has now been demolished.

Pugin was indirectly responsible for a church in GLASGOW. At the request of his former client, the banker Henry Drummond, in 1850 or thereabouts, he supplied drawings for a building for the CATHOLIC APOSTOLIC CHURCH, the recondite sect founded by the extraordinary Scots

St Mary's R.C. Church in Liverpool on its second site in Highfield Street, photographed in the late 19th century.

charismatic preacher, Edward Irving. This was built in McAslin Street –in 1852 – by the Glasgow architect James Salmon, without Pugin's supervision. Although not so large or as sumptuous as the surviving Irvingite church in Gordon Square, London, the building was long and noble, with tall arcades leading to an apsidal chancel.

The expected Second Coming having not yet occurred, the Catholic Apostolic Church waned in the 20th century and the altar of the Glasgow church was ceremonially broken in 1957 and the congregation dispersed. The fate of the building was then inevitable and typical; as Frank Worsdall wrote, 'Oblivious to its supreme importance in the history of both the architectural and religious life of this country, Glasgow Corporation demolished it in 1970'.[65]

Because of the fissiparous tendency of

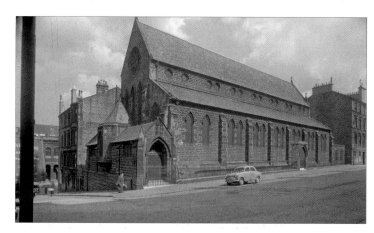

The exterior of the Catholic Apostolic Church in Glasgow in 1963.

Presbyterianism, Scottish cities were furnished with a superfluity of churches (with confusing names) in the Victorian period. Regardless of architectural quality, many have since disappeared – particularly in GLASGOW. The RENFIELD STREET UNITED PRESBYTERIAN CHURCH stood in the city centre, on the corner of Renfield Street and Sauchiehall Street, and was ambitious in scale, often known as 'The United Presbyterian Cathedral'. The church was designed by James Brown in a spiky Gothic manner which, when it opened in 1848, was old fashioned by English ecclesiological standards, but it was a delightful building – particularly inside, where ribbed plaster vaults and galleries on three sides were supported on very thin iron columns. Frank Worsdall recalled,

> it was one of the few city churches to keep its doors open during the week for shoppers and passers-by to spend a few minutes in prayer or meditation. Eventually the congregation found it too difficult to maintain the building, and it was sold reluctantly for redevelopment and demolished in 1965.[66]

At the beginning of his career, the prolific George Gilbert Scott had been converted to the ideal of building 'correct' Gothic churches by reading Pugin, whose 'articles excited me almost to fury'.[67] Subsequently, his office produced designs for a large number of churches – perhaps

▲ The interior of the Catholic Apostolic Church in Glasgow, photographed by David Walker.

too many – and while many of these are rather pedestrian, some are, or were, magnificent. For, inevitably, several of Scott's many churches have perished. HOLY TRINITY CHURCH in the centre of RUGBY was one of his better works.

Built in 1852–54, it was designed in the architect's favourite Geometrical Decorated style and had a crossing tower. The church was declared

◀ The Renfield Street United Presbyterian Church in Glasgow in 1963.

▶ The glorious galleried interior of the Renfield Street United Presbyterian Church in Glasgow in 1964, shortly before it was destroyed.

redundant in 1974 and several years of disgraceful neglect followed before a draft redundancy scheme for its demolition was announced in 1979. As Holy Trinity was listed, at Grade A, the first non-statutory public inquiry into a scheme to demolish an Anglican church was held the following year, at which the Victorian Society as well as local objectors gave evidence. In the course of this it emerged that half the estimated repair bill of £100,000 was due to neglect of maintenance by the Diocese of Coventry – which chose to be absent from the inquiry.

The result, announced the following year, was that the Inspector did not feel able, within the terms of the 1968 Pastoral Measure, to refuse to allow demolition, but recommended a 12-month delay to allow a local action group to negotiate with the Church Commissioners and to raise funds to preserve the building. The Secretary of State recommended categorically that the building should not be demolished. But the following year, 1981, Holy Trinity was demolished: the delinquent Diocese clearly could not wait to get the building down.

In LEEDS, two remarkable Victorian churches disappeared just before the Second World War as part of slum clearance schemes. One, the Church of St John the Evangelist, was modelled on the Temple Church in London by Scott, but no photographs of it seem to have survived. Another was by that most original and perverse of the

The exterior and interior of Holy Trinity Church in Rugby, photographed in 1978.

Victorian 'hards' (as W.R. Lethaby called them), William Butterfield. This was ST THOMAS'S CHURCH in Melbourne Street in Leeds, an early essay in his distinctive brick polychromatic manner. The nave was built in 1849–52, the chancel following in 1890–93. The exterior was a tough composition, built in a tough area. In 1854, the *Ecclesiologist* described how,

> Standing in a squalid waste, strewed with heaps of rubbish, St Thomas stands out as

unmistakeably a town church. Mr Butterfield always seems to build *con amore*, where there are extraordinary difficulties; and he succeeds with bricks better, in proportion, than with any other material.[68]

Fortunately, John Summerson photographed the exterior of this long-lost building shortly before it disappeared and Henry-Russell Hitchcock went to see it, later describing how,

The polychrome brick exterior of St Thomas's in Leeds, photographed by John Summerson in the late 1930s and later published by Henry-Russell Hitchcock and the interior of the church, from a postcard.

▲▶ The exterior of All Saints' Clifton in Bristol photographed by V. Turl after bomb damage and the interior of the church as it looked in 1928.

The plain billets of stone set between the horizontal bands lower down produce a crisp pattern suggesting abstract paintings of the 1920's. The red bricks remained cleaner here than in London, despite the general grime of Leeds, and were of a light orange-pink tone. The headers, moreover, were of a pale blue-gray, lighter than the stone bands. The wilful destruction of this edifice, long dismantled, removed a major work from the Butterfieldian canon.[69]

ALL SAINTS', CLIFTON, BRISTOL, was another highly original, High Victorian Gothic church that has gone – this time as the result of enemy action, although it could – and should – have been restored. Designed in 1863 by George Edmund Street, later the architect of the Law Courts in London, the church was an experiment in adapting Mediaeval forms for ritualistic worship. The nave was wide, for large congregations; the chancel much narrower. To concentrate attention on the chancel, the nave was made tough and simple, with powerful arches rising from squat, simple piers. The aisles were but passages, formed by transverse vaults expressed on the exterior as a row of gables. A particularly remarkable feature was the way the easternmost bay of the nave arcades suddenly leapt up higher, only for the arch to collide with the chancel arch wall in mid-flight. All Saints' was ready by 1880, although the unfinished tower with only its octagonal belfry, designed by F.C. Eden, in

1926–27. In 1940, the roof was burned off by incendiary bombs. The following decade Pevsner wrote, 'That this church was gutted in the Second World War is a major loss to Victorian church architecture. All Saints was a mature work of a serious and self-confident architect, rarely satisfied with the copying of old motifs and elements'.[70]

Street's tough stone walls and arcades still stood, however, and the building could easily have been re-roofed. But the architect Robert Potter declared they were beyond repair and replaced them with a new church, retaining only the stump of Street's tower and his narthex. So eventually, as Andor Gomme later wrote,

in a worse catastrophe in 1964, the shell of the church itself was destroyed – an irreparable and needless loss, comparable in value with that of St Peter's Hospital, which no merits in its successor can compensate: All Saints' was Bristol's most distinguished Victorian building, one of Street's very finest churches, a piece of creative architectural thinking of rare quality.[71]

There was little possibility of restoring ST FAITH'S, STOKE NEWINGTON, in London, for in 1944 a V1 destroyed most of the western parts of the church to leave half the west wall standing as a jagged fragment. St Faith's was designed in a tough, Early French style by William Burges, that most romantic of Victorian Goths. It had an apsidal end and narrow passage aisles, with a sort of tall

◀ St Faith's, Stoke Newington, in north-east London photographed by Dell & Wainwright for the Architectural Press shortly after it was half demolished by a flying bomb in 1944.

triforium or gallery above them behind iron columns, supporting the upper wall and roof. Most of the church was built between 1871–73, but the severe and simple west end only completed in 1881–82 by James Brooks after Burges's death.

Following the bombing, a dramatic photograph was taken of the half-demolished church for the National Buildings Record. John Summerson then used it as the frontispiece of his 1949 book of essays, *Heavenly Mansions*, and, in discussing the preservation of ruins, noted how when the flying-bomb destroyed the west end of St Faith's,

> a spectacle of incredible grandeur was created out of a church of very moderate artistic stature. It became a torso – the fragment of something infinitely magnificent. The remote apse was patinaed with sunlight sprayed through open rafters; and the west wall had been torn aside just sufficiently for the noble and still fresh interior to gain by contrast with its rough-hewn shell. Nothing could have been

more moving – and nothing less stable. The ruin of St Faith's will remain a fine thing until it is removed; but the brilliance of the first revelation has gone for ever.[72]

And today, of course, the ruin has long since been cleared.

ST CLEMENT'S, SHEEPSCAR, in Leeds was one of many redundant churches helped into extinction by local arsonists. A substantial church in a French Gothic style designed by the local Leeds architect George Corson, St Clement's was built in 1867–68. Comprehensive redevelopment of the surrounding area in the 1960s eliminated the congregation and led to the church's closure. The building was declared redundant in 1975, although it had been listed the previous year. Soon after closure, during the 'waiting period' required under the Church of England's Pastoral Measure, St Clement's was badly damaged by fire and it was demolished the following year.

One of the most intriguing of Victorian church

▲▶ The derelict and vandalised exterior and interior of St Clement's, Sheepscar, in Leeds in 1975 shortly before demolition.

architects was Samuel Sanders Teulon, whose work revealed a strong attempt at originality within the vigorous High Victorian aesthetic. Two of his extraordinary London churches (St Stephen's, Rosslyn Hill, Hampstead and St Mark's Silvertown) have managed to survive against the odds, but two more perished after the Second World War.

ST ANDREW'S, COIN STREET, was built in 1855–56 on a site near Waterloo Station. Influenced by Butterfield's All Saints', Margaret Street, then rising, Teulon's rather Germanic-looking church was remarkable for its patterned brickwork, with horizontal bands of London stock bricks alternating with hammer-dressed 'greystone' rising from the ground right up the tower. A timber spire rose above this tower, which had more patterned brickwork in its triangular gables, and at the base the entrance was surmounted by an odd and elaborate traceried window typical of the architect. St Andrew's was badly damaged by bombs and demolished in the 1950s.

ST THOMAS'S, WROTHAM ROAD, near Camden Town, was possibly Teulon's strangest and most original church. It was a replacement of an earlier church also by Teulon, built a little further south. St Thomas's, Agar Town was a centrally planned building, designed in 1857 but it was not even finished when the site was acquired for a proposed terminus at St Pancras by the Midland Railway.

With the help of compensation from the railway company, the new St Thomas's was more ambitious.

▶ ▶▶ The exterior and west door of St Andrew's, Coin Street, near Waterloo Bridge photographed in 1944 during the Second World War.

Consecrated in 1863, it was built of brick and had two transepts as well as an apsidal east end. Over the crossing rose a massive square tower which mutated into an octagon, capped by a squat spire. The design reflected the High Victorian interest in basic – and powerful – geometrical forms.

Pevsner, in 1951, rather missed the point by writing that the church was, 'Immensely coarse, the tracery amongst the grossest, least correct in London'. A decade or so later, however – in 1964 – Paul Thompson, in trying to assess 'The High Victorian Cultural Achievement' for the newly founded Victorian Society, could describe it as a 'Masterpiece in "ugliness": a defiant slum church . . .'[73] Unfortunately, by then this extraordinary building had disappeared. Damaged in the Second World War, it was eventually demolished in about 1960.

In his celebrated lecture on 'Rogue Architects of the Victorian Era', H.S. Goodhart-Rendel identified a number of nonconformist architects who, like rogue-elephants, were 'driven or living apart from the herd, and of savage temper'. One of them was Enoch Bassett Keeling who, in addition to the long-lost, once-notorious Strand Music Hall, was responsible for six churches in London. Rendel disliked them; 'There is no question of their being beautiful, but they try very hard to be amusing and it may be my fault that they do not amuse me'.[74] They also tried hard to be original, in High Victorian Gothic terms, as well as to provide a space for Low rather than High Church worship by using thin, cast-iron columns and installing galleries – anathema to many ecclesiologists.

ST PAUL'S, PENGE, or Upper Norwood, was built in 1864–66 and had a richly decorated stencilled interior with Gothic arcades on iron columns with almost a Moorish character. As James Stevens Curl has observed, by

> using factory methods, repetitive designs, and ultra-simple joinery, Keeling achieved the richest of effects, which may not have been truly 'mediaeval', but which attained a character of some interest at a fraction of the cost of the buildings of his more acceptable ecclesiologist-minded contemporaries.[75]

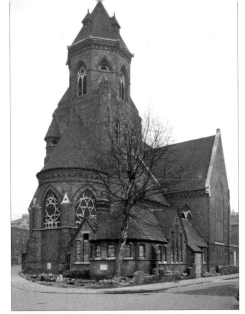

▲ The extraordinary, defiantly eccentric exterior of Teulon's St Thomas's Church near Camden Town photographed by Sydney Newbery in c.1952.

▼ The Paul's Church in Hamlet Road, Penge, in 1970.

▶ The interior of St Paul's Penge, in 1970, still in fine condition but to be demolished soon afterwards.

St Paul's was threatened with closure in 1969, eventually closed in 1971 and was demolished a year later after the statutory 'waiting period' of a year. As the Victorian Society complained,

> in such circumstances a year is simply not long enough to investigate all possibilities, and had the Church Commissioners not been in such a hurry an alternative use might well have been found.[76]

ST JUDE'S, GRAY'S INN ROAD was designed by Joseph Peacock, another of Rendel's 'rogues'. Consecrated in 1863, it was the first church built in London with the aid of the Bishop of London's Fund established by Archibald Tait, the future Archbishop of Canterbury. Such beneficence may have been ill-advised, however, as the church has since disappeared – not because of enemy action in the Second World War but earlier, through the rationalisation of parishes in St Pancras.

Fortunately, its exterior was recorded by John Summerson shortly before it disappeared in 1936. This may have been because, with its thin saddle-back tower and unusual tracery, it was a good example of its architect's eccentric Gothic manner. The Revd Basil Clarke remembered it as 'a church in which Peacock let

◀ ▲ Two views of the exterior of St Jude's, Gray's Inn Road, taken by John Summerson in 1936 shortly before demolition.

himself go' while for Goodhart-Rendel, 'that *was* fun – that was!'[77]

Goodhart-Rendel also considered Alexander 'Greek' Thomson to be a rogue as he resolutely rejected the fashion for Gothic and pursued his own personal Greek style. But he was much more than a provincial nonconformist; Thomson was a true original and Henry-Russell Hitchcock considered that he designed 'three of the finest Romantic Classical churches in the world' in GLASGOW. Of these, one and a half survive (for the Caledonia Road Church is now but a gutted ruin).

The one that has gone – Scotland's worst architectural loss of the Second World War – was the QUEEN'S PARK CHURCH. Built in 1868–69, this modern temple for a United Presbyterian congregation was wholly unconventional in both style and structure. The exterior was Egyptian as much as Greek in style and its front was surmounted by a strange Indian-looking dome above the pediment. The interior astonished all who saw it: galleries and clerestory were supported on exotic iron columns; the large windows, of sheet and coloured glass, were applied directly to the masonry and, over the entrance, parallel strips of glazing ran between and independent of the columns, both stone and iron – a feature which might seem to anticipate the work of Frank Lloyd Wright in Chicago.

The whole was treated with a gorgeous scheme of stencilled decoration executed in collaboration with Daniel Cottier. Photographs suggest that the raised platform for the minister's desk flanked by Egyptian doors and with a gallery above was not unlike an sacrificial altar in a set by Cecil B. DeMille for, say, *Cleopatra*. When he saw inside in 1883, the Pre-Raphaelite painter Ford Madox Brown exclaimed,

> I want nothing better than the religion that produced art like that. Here line and colouring are suggestive of Paradise itself. Well done Glasgow! I put this Thomson-Cottier church above everything I have seen in modern Europe.[78]

In one of the last German air raids on the Clyde, in 1943 the Queen's Park Church was hit by incendiary bombs. Because there had been a plasterers' strike when the church was built, the interior was entirely lined with wood, which burned fiercely and this amazing building was totally destroyed.

ST ENOCH'S FREE CHURCH in Partick, GLASGOW was perhaps Scotland's second-worst architectural loss in the Second World War. Unlike

▲ ▶ The interior of the Queen's Park Church in Glasgow soon after the installation of an organ in 1881 and two photographs, one showing the interior looking towards the entrance, commissioned by Henry-Russell Hitchcock from T. & R. Annan in 1936.

Thomson's masterpiece, St Enoch's was Gothic. It was designed by one of Glasgow's best Victorian architects, James Sellars, of the firm of Campbell Douglas & Sellars, who had won a competition in 1873. The triangular site in Old Dumbarton Road was awkward, but the church was cleverly planned. A church hall was set across the widest part of the triangle and a tall tower with a crown-steeple placed at the apex. The church was badly damaged during one of the German air raids on the Clyde and subsequently demolished.

Just as not all Victorian churches were Gothic, so many did not have a conventional plan with chancel, nave and aisles. One such was NOTRE

DAME DE FRANCE, the French Roman Catholic church in LONDON. The church was circular in plan as it had originally been the Rotunda designed by Robert Mitchell and built in 1793–94, just off Leicester Square, for Robert Barker's Panorama. The space within the brick walls was converted into a church in 1865–68 by the French architect, Louis-Auguste Boileau, best known for the church of St Eugène in Paris, with its remarkable Gothic interior constructed in cast-iron.

Boileau's London church also employed iron construction and he placed within the circle a rectilinear arrangement of cast-iron piers, arches and ribs. The effect was not beautiful but certainly extraordinary. In 1940, the church was damaged but repaired; only to be demolished a decade later to be replaced by the present building of 1951–55, designed by Hector Corfiato (also circular in plan).

Many, perhaps most, of the famous and best Victorian churches were Anglican and designed by well-known architects, but it is important to remember that these, in numerical terms, were a minority and that many chapels – very different in both style and plan – were built by the Nonconformist churches. And, because these organisations have had no internal system of control for dealing with buildings of architectural interest, many of them have been demolished,

St Enoch's Free Church in Partick, Glasgow, in 1966.

often without much thought for alternative use and without being properly recorded.

A particularly fine example of the type of large Nonconformist chapel – essentially a large, galleried auditorium – once so common in the North of England was the BOLD STREET CHAPEL in WARRINGTON, Lancashire. Built in 1850 for a

◀ ◀◀ The circular interior of the French Roman Catholic church of Notre Dame de France.

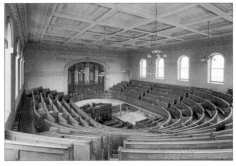

▲▶ The entrance front and the galleried interior of the Bold Street Chapel in Warrington, Lancashire, in 1971.

Methodist congregation, it was designed by James Simpson of Leeds. In *The Fall of Zion*, a book published by SAVE Britain's Heritage in 1980 to draw attention to the plight of Northern chapel architecture, Ken Powell wrote,

> Simpson was an architect of genuine stature who produced an inventive series of variations on some basic themes. Bold Street Chapel which had Simpson's customary twin doorways, had an interior rightly described by [Peter] Fleetwood-Hesketh as 'magnificent'. The plasterwork and woodwork were of the highest quality and the whole ensemble was almost unchanged.

Yet the building was demolished in the early 1970s – not because it was redundant but to be replaced by a multi-purpose brick box containing a hall and chapel.

Nonconformist architecture continues to be vulnerable. The TABERNACLE CALVINISTIC METHODIST CHAPEL in the centre of ABERYSTWYTH was a fine example of the huge chapels which are such typical landmarks in Welsh towns. Built in 1878–79, it was the fourth – and last – chapel on the site since 1785. It had a vast and impressive galleried interior and a stone-arched façade in a style that its architect, Richard Owens, called 'Italo-Lombard'.

Closed in 2002, the chapel stood empty but was bought by a local developer and garage-owner who secured planning permission to convert the interior into flats. In 2008, the building went on fire. The blaze was so fierce that local residents had to be evacuated and by the following morning the listed building was a gutted shell. At first CADW, the Welsh historic

▼▶ The exterior of the Tabernacle Calvinistic Methodist Chapel in Aberystwyth photographed by Penny Icke in 1996 and the galleried interior taken by Ian Wright in 1998.

buildings agency, insisted the façade be retained, but the developer persuaded Ceredigion County Council that the ruin was unstable. What remained of the Tabernacle Chapel was rapidly demolished a week later, the speed of its disappearance causing much upset in the town.

Many Nonconformist places of worship continued the Georgian tradition in both style and planning, if with greater ornament and elaboration. As the century advanced, however, Gothic was increasingly employed. Some architects merely adopted both the style and plan of ecclesiologically-correct Anglican churches, as demanded by fashion, but some more interesting and inventive architects tried to adapt Gothic to the rather different requirements of Nonconformist worship. In particular, James Cubitt in England, like F.T. Pilkington in Scotland, exploited the freedom and flexibility of Gothic to create centrally-planned churches with unorthodox internal spaces unlike anything imagined or approved of by Pugin and his disciples.

In his book on *Church Design for Congregations: Its Development and Possibilities*, published in 1870, Cubitt argued, 'our thirteenth century predecessors surrounded their own forms of worship with an architecture as characteristic as it is grand – they would have devised an equally characteristic one for ours'. He put his ideas most famously into effect in the Union Chapel in Islington, an ambitious building with a large, octagonal central space, with galleries behind the Gothic arches. Despite threats of closure and demolition, this magnificent building survives, but other examples of Cubitt's resourcefulness have perished.

One such was the cathedral-like CHURCH OF THE REDEEMER, built in 1881–82, in the Hagley Road, for the Baptists of BIRMINGHAM. Early English in style, it enclosed a large central space under a central tower with a tall octagonal lantern, flanked by transepts. Nonconformity's historian, Clyde Binfield, has written how

> The Redeemer was marked by its lantern-towered crossing space, defined by massive stone columns. The gallery was believed to run counter to Cubitt's wishes and was generally held to weaken the interior's firm lines. Even so, here again was 'Architecture in the New Spirit', neither Bethel nor Mount Zion but a church 'that might, to all seeming, have been in use by any religious body in almost any age'.[79]

Unfortunately, forward-looking as Cubitt's centralised plans might seem, this grand Baptist church was demolished in 1975.

Synagogues of architectural distinction have also proved to extremely vulnerable, owing both to cultural reasons and the independence of

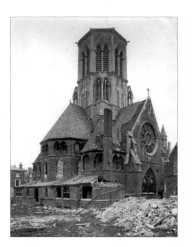

◀◀ ◀ The Church of the Redeemer in Birmingham: the exterior and interior in 1975 when demolition had commenced.

congregations. As Sharman Kadish, the historian and campaigner for the Jewish architectural heritage, has lamented,

> Enormous physical destruction has already taken place. Synagogues have fallen victim to wartime bombing or, more usually, to Jewish demographic shift and urban renewal. The contraction of Anglo-Jewry nationwide and its increasing centralization in suburban London and Manchester mean that the future of several more of our dwindling stock of fine Victorian synagogues must be in doubt.

However,

> Experience has taught us that listing, if carried out early enough, may serve as a deterrent against asset-stripping by synagogue organisations and the predatory intentions of property developers.[80]

A major loss was the GREAT SYNAGOGUE in Cheetham Hill, MANCHESTER, designed by Thomas Bird and built in 1857–58 for the city's Ashkenazi community. 'This imposing building, with a marble-clad façade upon a brick body, should not have surprised anyone who knew about the role of the Jews, especially those of German origin, in developing the city in the mid-nineteenth century', wrote Carol Krinsky.

> This synagogue was built about the same time as those of Paris [1852], Mannheim [1855], Hamburg [1857], Brno [1855] and Budapest [1859]. It could only have surprised others accustomed only to the pseudo-Moorish and eclectic synagogues typical of a later generation . . . the lower floor, entered behind a vestibule, appeared as stately and spacious as a town hall or large dissenting church . . .[81]

(Bird had earlier designed Cheetham Town Hall). The Great Synagogue was closed when the Jewish community moved away from the Cheetham Hill area. Although a listed building and the subject of a long campaign by the Manchester Group of the Victorian Society, 'the synagogue had been systematically run down by its recent owners and was eventually demolished as a dangerous structure' in 1986.[82]

To return to Anglican churches and to London, ST JOHN'S, RED LION SQUARE was one of the finest of the mature creations of J.L. Pearson. Built in 1874–78, of red brick and stone in the architect's favourite Normandy Gothic, it was remarkable for being vaulted throughout and having a chancel

narrower than the nave in the manner of Gerona Cathedral in Spain. John Summerson considered, 'it displayed a mastery of the art of stone vaulting never seen since the Middle Ages'.

The church was severely damaged by bombs in 1941. 'St John's has been blown to pieces,' wrote Summerson the following year, 'and since that event ruthless demolition has taken place. But Pearson's drawings exist, and it would hardly be mistaken piety to bring this church back to its former perfection'.[83] Others thought that, with the blasted arcades and springing of the vaults left open to the sky, the church made a magnificent ruin.

In a pamphlet on 'Bombed Churches As War Memorials', published by the Architectural Press in 1945, it was argued,

▶ The glorious vaulted interior of Pearson's masterpiece in Red Lion Square in 1890.

Enough of it remains for it to be re-created as a garden ruin. It is proposed that the ruin be united to the garden in the square by closing off the subsidiary road which now separates them from each other, and by planting the intervening space with an avenue of trees. This eventually would complete the perspective looking down the ruined choir of the church.

Pevsner agreed, writing a few years later that this 'very impressive ruin should be preserved as a memorial ruin'.[84] Needless to say, this did not happen. The site of St John's was cleared and in 1961 a new road driven across the west side of the square, in front of where Pearson's masterpiece had stood.

Another great church of the 1870s, ST AGNES', KENNINGTON PARK, was also damaged in the Second World War but, unlike St John's, could easily have been restored. Built in 1874–91, St Agnes' was the masterpiece of George Gilbert Scott junior, the brilliant, troubled son of Sir

Gilbert Scott. It was one of the most influential of Late-Victorian churches, for Scott had challenged the mid-Victorian prejudice against Late Gothic. With its furnishings intended for Anglo-Catholic worship and stained glass by C.E. Kempe, the church had a Continental air. The ecclesiologist Francis Bumpus wrote,

> with its magnificent screens, stained glass, altarpieces, roof paintings, graceful arcades and ample chair-seated area, [it] might be taken for a church built during the palmist days of the Early Perpendicular period by some wealthy wool-stapler who had brought with him reminiscences of Flanders.[85]

St Agnes' was still regarded as 'modern' and a model for emulation in the 1920s. In 1941 the timber roof was burned off by incendiary bombs; the fittings were all rescued, but the shell left to stand open to the weather. In 1946, Stephen Dykes Bower, the architect charged with the church's restoration, reported that what survived represented

The interior of St Agnes', Kennington Park, in 1901 and the exterior of the church, with Scott's vicarage placed across the west end, in the 1920s.

75% of the cost of rebuilding. The Diocese of Southwark had other ideas, however, and in 1953 a new vicar decided to replace Scott's church with something smaller. The following year, the chairman of the Central Council for the Care of Churches informed the War Damage Commission that,

> we feel that this church may be considered the most important 19th century building to have been damaged in the late war, and we suggest that it deserves special treatment.[86]

All Hallows', Southwark, seen from the south-east after bomb damage during the Second World War.

The Commission agreed and offered to pay for full restitution but, shamefully, the Diocese used the money to demolish the ruins of the church in 1956 and build an unworthy replacement. John Betjeman, who had fought hard to save St Agnes', dedicated his *Collins Guide to English Parish Churches* (1958) to the memory of two 'fine churches of unfashionable date demolished since the war' – one of which was St Agnes', Kennington.

St Michael's, Folkestone, from the north-east in the late 19th century.

Poor Scott was unlucky as his other important London church also perished as a result of the Second World War. ALL HALLOWS', SOUTHWARK, was an Anglo-Catholic mission church built in 1878–92, not far south of Southwark Bridge to minister to the inhabitants of a notorious slum. Inside, Scott's typical refined arcades led to a narrower chancel and there were dramatic changes in floor level. Outside, the church presented a bleak outline and austere composition of red brick walls, an example of what the social reformer Charles Booth called 'the bare style' so typical of High Victorian urban churches. Francis Bumpus thought, 'The view of All Hallows' from the south-east is, I am bold to say, one of the finest things in the whole range of modern architecture'.[87]

In 1941 the south side was damaged by bombs then, three years later, the west end of the church was largely destroyed by a flying bomb. Eventually, the whole building was demolished to make a small park, except for the Morning Chapel to the northeast, which was incorporated into a miserable new church – and made redundant in 1971.

Along with the younger Scott, George Frederick Bodley was the architect who did most to change the direction of the Gothic Revival away from Continental-inspired vigour and towards a more English refinement in Late Gothic forms. A forgotten church in FOLKESTONE, Kent, dedicated to ST MICHAEL, was a fine and cleverly planned example, designed in collaboration with his partner, Thomas Garner. Begun in 1872, it was a difficult commission owing both to the awkward, sloping, triangular site and the vicious religious politics of the town, for St Michael's was designed for Anglo-Catholic worship. A nave and chancel were built first, with a single, separate north aisle with a tower completed by 1884. The plan was as ingenious as the treatment of the Late Gothic style was elegant.

In 1940, the church was closed when Folkestone, like other seaside towns threatened with invasion, was evacuated. Although it suffered only minor war damage, it never re-opened. The lingering prejudice against ritualism,

which also seems to have affected the fate of Scott's two London churches, resulted in it being demolished in 1953. The thin octagonal steeple which enhanced this remarkable building had to be removed with the assistance of dynamite.

By the end of Victoria's reign, Bodley was Britain's best known and most respected ecclesiastical architect; Norman Shaw wrote that he was 'beyond all doubt the most accomplished and refined architect in Europe' and before his death in 1906 he would be asked to design cathedrals in both Washington, DC, and San Francisco.[88]

ST EDWARD'S, HOLBECK, was a notably fine example of his work. Built in 1902–04 as an Anglo-Catholic mission church in LEEDS, it had an interior with nave and aisles bisected by an elaborate screen and elegant arcades leading to a windowless east wall, against which stood one of the architect's splendid reredoses, Late Gothic in style. Owing to population movements in the city, St Edward's was closed in 1976, and then boarded up and abandoned. This noble, beautiful building was eventually demolished in 1984.

JEZREEL'S TOWER at GILLINGHAM in Kent might well be regarded as the most extraordinary building to emerge from Victorian Britain. Often described as a folly, this huge, if incomplete structure was the product of serious intent and testified to the continuing vitality of fringe millenarian sects throughout the 19th century.

The tower, or temple, was the brainchild of

▶ ▶▶ Jezreel's Tower at Gillingham in Kent: the exterior as completed, from an early 20th century postcard, and as it looked when photographed by Edwin Smith in 1957.

James Roland White, a soldier based at Chatham, who in 1875 took over the leadership of the New House of Israel, a group of British-Israelites who were descendents of the followers of Joanna Southcott and her Box, and who believed in the imminent Second Coming and that only a small number of the elect would be saved. White declared himself the 'Messenger of the Lord', changed his name to James Jershom Jezreel and wrote down his prophesies in a document known as the *Flying Roll*.

The tower to be built near the top of Chatham Hill was intended as the headquarters of his sect. Jezreel wanted it to be a perfect cube, with sides 144ft long, but his architect, William Margetts of Chatham, persuaded him this was impractical and in the event, the building was to be 120ft high, with sides 124ft 6in long. It was constructed of yellow brick, steel and concrete. Eight projecting square towers rising to battlements – one at each corner and one in the middle of each side – gave the tower something of the appearance of an Elizabethan prodigy castle. Symbols of the New and Latter House of Israel, including the *Flying Roll*, were placed on the walls. Inside was to be a huge, circular assembly hall, lit by electricity and

covered by a 94ft diameter glass dome, rising almost the full height of the building; in the middle of this was to be a circular revolving platform, for choir and preachers, which could be raised and lowered by hydraulic power.

Work on the tower began in 1885 when, unfortunately, Jezreel died. By 1888, when his wife and successor, known as 'Queen Esther', followed him, the money had run out and building work stopped. The exterior walls had been built almost their full height, but the roofless interior was just a tangle of steel girders. The few remaining followers of the church lost control of its unfinished temple, which reverted to the firm that built it. In 1905, new owners decided to take down the upper floors but the builder entrusted with the demolition went bankrupt and the tower survived for over half a century as an extraordinary forlorn jagged shell. It attracted the attention of, among others, the Surrealist painter Tristram Hillier (1905–83), who painted it as a poster for Shell petrol in 1936.

In the 1950s, Olive Cook and Edwin Smith, in search of follies, found it, 'an astonishing spectacle in its present surroundings of allotments and little villas'.[89] In 1959, the Gillingham Co-operative society, which had

bought the premises in 1920 so the adjacent buildings along Canterbury Street could be used as shops, offered the tower to Gillingham Town Council for a nominal sum so that it could be preserved as a unique historical relic. The blinkered Council declined the offer, so it was then sold to a local industrialist, who wanted to build an electro-plating works on the site. So this extraordinary landmark – by far the most interesting building in the area – was demolished in 1960–61. 'Even those who regarded its advent with scepticism, back in 1885, could hardly have imagined that the great tower would not last a century and that it would be pulled down efficiently and dispassionately, without protest from a generation which had become conditioned tamely to accept the gradual destruction of England's heritage of beautiful or strange buildings'.[90]

7: PUBLIC BUILDINGS

Victorian public buildings were built to last. Monumental expressions of civic or national pride, they were solidly constructed, richly embellished and intended to serve a purpose that would endure. Few major Victorian public buildings have in fact been demolished, much as town councillors and others might have wished to replace them when they were out of fashion, and today the great 19th-century town halls of Northern cities remain as much a focus of civic pride as they ever were, although some were rendered redundant by the endless reorganisations of local government, which characterised the second half of the 20th century in Britain.

Apart from the ones that have perished by accident or enemy action, those that have gone were victims of the prejudice against Victorian architecture when utilitarian considerations were allowed to intervene. Victorian buildings had no place in the utopian post-war world dreamed up by town-planners and road engineers.

The TOWN HALL in KINGSTON-UPON-HULL made a surprisingly early disappearance. The result of a typically mismanaged competition held in 1861, it was designed by a local boy, Cuthbert Brodrick, best known for his buildings in Leeds,

above all the stupendous Classical town hall. Rather smaller was the town hall in the East Riding port. The exterior was in a Venetian Renaissance manner, with columns of red Mansfield stone dividing arcaded bays on two floors. In the centre of the elevation facing was a projecting entrance, above which rose a clock tower. This rose to a two-storey cupola. When the building was taken down in 1911, this cupola was re-erected in a local park. Brodrick's biographer notes that

> its appearance is curiously similar to the type of small mausoleum or garden pavilion such as one finds in Northern India. For a moment one can imagine one is in the Lodi Gardens in New Delhi, and not in Pearson Park, leading him to speculate on an Oriental influence on his architecture.[91]

Hull's town hall was largely an administrative building, with no public hall. Brodrick's only opportunity for architectural effects internally was in the staircase hall and the mayor's reception room. The former was embellished with

◀◀ Gilbert Scott's proud new Town Hall for Preston, Lancashire, photographed in c.1935.

▶ Hull's long-demolished Guildhall, photographed by Frith & Co. in 1903.

various stones and marbles in different colours: buff, white, grey, red and green.

'Talk of Athens, pride of Greece, / Talk of Venice, talk of Nice, / The Town Hall, Hull, in Lowgate stands, / Competing with those classic lands / In architectural beauty . . .' wrote a local poet.[92] Because the town hall was small, a competition for an extension containing law courts and a council chamber was held in 1903. This was won by the young Edwin Cooper. Once completed, it was decided to demolish Brodrick's building and replace it by a grand entrance front more in keeping with the new building, so different and more refined did Edwardian Baroque seem to be when compared with ebullient mid-Victorian Classicism. Other pieces of Brodrick's building found their way to the village of Brantingham.

PRESTON TOWN HALL, Gothic rather than Classic, fell victim to fire, not taste. Built in 1862–67, it was designed by George Gilbert Scott in the secular Gothic style he had proposed in vain for the new Government Offices in Whitehall, and which would be realised on a larger scale at the Midland Grand Hotel at St Pancras Station. Like the Midland Hotel, Preston Town Hall had a corner clock tower with a spire. Scott recorded that his style at Preston had a French character and that the building had particularly large windows; as always, he was anxious to emphasise the practicality and modernity of his secular Gothic.

Preston Town Hall was gutted by fire in March 1947. The roof was burned off and the clock tower very badly damaged. Subsequently, the

◀◀ ▲ ◀ Preston Town Hall, seen from Fishergate in the 1930s and two photographs of its Gothic interior taken in c.1935.

tower and part of the walls were taken down to make the ruin safe. Some repairs were carried out, but despite £140,000 of insurance money being available, no serious attempt was made to restore Scott's building, which stood as a ruin throughout the 1950s. Eventually, despite considerable public protest, the town council decided to demolish what remained and the site was cleared in 1962. Its replacement – Crystal House, of 1963 – is a far less worthy neighbour to the fine Classical civic buildings on the north side of the Market Place.

HOUNSLOW TOWN HALL and LIBRARY were once the only buildings of any real character in a village that has been swallowed up by west

▶ Hounslow Town Hall in c.1965.

London. Council house, library and public baths were combined in a group of buildings erected in 1904–05 by Hounlow & Isleworth Urban District Council, just off Hounslow High Street. All were designed by T. Nowell Parr, a local municipal architect later specialising in public houses.

Parr's buildings were vaguely Art Nouveau in style and built of red brick, terra-cotta and ceramic. They were rendered redundant when Hounslow Borough Council built a new Civic Centre nearby, in 1965–75. The Council then decided to sacrifice them to a new shopping centre it was promoting. Demolition was opposed by the Victorian Society and the Ancient Monuments Society, and the case went to public inquiry in 1980. The Greater London Council equivocated and attended the inquiry simply to give historical evidence.

In the event, the Secretary of State granted permission for demolition; as the Victorian Society reported in 1981, 'Hounslow will be the poorer for the loss of Parr's cheerful terracotta buildings'. This is certainly the case; as Bridget Cherry later concluded about the Treaty Centre, a shopping centre containing a library built in 1984–87, 'The result is the sadder because this great hulk replaced a distinguished group of civic buildings in Treaty Road . . .'[93]

The IMPERIAL INSTITUTE in South Kensington was the first major undamaged Victorian building to be demolished after the Second World War and its arguably unnecessary destruction emphasised the need to protect the best Victorian architecture. The Institute was a consequence of the successful Indian and Colonial Exhibition held in South Kensington in 1886 and was built by public subscription as a memorial to Queen Victoria's Golden Jubilee, celebrated the following year.

A limited competition, held in 1887, was won by Thomas Edward Collcutt and the principal part of his design opened in 1893. Magnificently built of red-gauged brickwork and Portland stone, it was the supreme example of the eclectic taste of the 1880s which Goodhart-Rendel characterised as 'Bric-à-brac'. It had, he wrote,

> not so much a French or Italian as a Spanish flavour at first peculiar to its architect, but afterwards, proving very much to the public taste, continued by a large number of his imitators . . . the whole building is a tour de force, combining as it does extreme delicacy of detail with breadth and grandeur in its general effect. The principal tower is extremely elegant in silhouette, admirably proportioned in itself, entirely useless for any known purpose . . .[94]

The Imperial Institute when new, photographed by Bedford Lemere in 1892; a view of the staircase in 1894 and one of the grand entrance hall by Herbert Felton in 1962.

Transferred to the Ministry of Education in 1949, Collcutt's masterpiece fell victim both to the retreat from Empire and new official interest in promoting science and progress. In 1953 – Coronation Year – the government decided to redevelop and expand the Imperial College of Science and Technology. This would involve demolishing several of the college's older buildings on its confined site between the Albert Hall and the Natural History Museum, including the excellent Royal School of Needlework by Fairfax B. Wade in Exhibition Road. The principal casualty was to be the Imperial Institute, although the Royal Fine Arts Commission, which complained of the secrecy and lack of open discussion surrounding the plans, remained unconvinced that Collcutt's building could not be retained in use.

Much controversy was engendered, particularly in the correspondence pages of *The Times*, after the proposals finally emerged into

▶ Birmingham Central Library
from the south in 1966.

the light of day in 1955. Objectors included architects both traditional and modern, ranging from Albert Richardson to Hugh Casson (see page 15). Many felt that the South Kensington site was the wrong one and that a modern science college should be built elsewhere. Goodhart-Rendel objected that no illustrations had been published of what was proposed to replace the buildings the government proposed to destroy and complained of the 'secrecy', which 'seems to have become lately an invariable cloak for important public works, which in former days needed some degree of public approval before they could be undertaken'. John Betjeman noted,

> If this masterpiece is to be taken down by the Government it will surely be the first time a British Government have committed such a crime for many years. It is hardly logical of
>
> Mr. Brooke [Financial Secretary to the Treasury] to equate the urgent need for scientists with the necessity for pulling down a fine piece of architecture.

Nor were all the objectors architects and writers; the scientist Julian Huxley pleaded that,

> Even if the main part of the existing building has to be destroyed, cannot the tower be retained, as a sign that even to-day other than purely utilitarian and technological values should carry weight in the planning of our cities?[95]

In the event, Collcutt's campanile *was* retained, albeit ineptly and incongruously, but there was no way of saving the rest; demolition commenced in 1956 and was completed by 1965. The replacement buildings, by Norman & Dawbarn, have never secured much critical admiration.

BIRMINGHAM CENTRAL LIBRARY was demolished not because it was redundant or impractical, but because it did not fit in with new civic vision that the car-obsessed city developed after the Second World War. The original building was designed by Edward Middleton Barry and consisted of the Birmingham and Midland Institute of 1855–57, which was extended with the contiguous Central Reference Library of 1863–65, designed by the local firm of Martin & Chamberlain; the two were united by an engaged Corinthian order. The opening of the library in 1866 was, as Asa Briggs has written, 'a great landmark in the history of the civic gospel'.[96] In 1879, it was gutted by fire and was

◀ The reading room of the Central Library in Birmingham, photographed in c.1933 by S. Smith.

then rebuilt by J.H. Chamberlain, who was responsible for the fine and spacious reading rooms, with their iron galleries and spiral staircases.

Next door was the Town Hall, a Corinthian temple designed in 1832, and nearby the City Museum of 1881–85 and the adjacent Council House of 1874–79; together they formed a fine 19th-century civic centre. In 1960, Ian Nairn observed how, with the Town Hall, the library

> makes an L-shaped pedestrian square, dotted with monuments and statues, that is a little masterpiece of Victorian urbanity. There is one spot under the portico of the library where all the buildings crowd together like a bit of orchestration by Bruckner or Mahler, and the whole of the nineteenth century can be apprehended like a revelation.[97]

In 1960 the City Council proposed a new Central Library immediately to the north, next to the Inner Ring Road. The Victorian Society fought hard for the consequent removal of the old library and the case went to public inquiry in 1973. The following year, the Secretary of State gave permission for its demolition, provided the special Shakespeare Memorial Room – 'probably the best surviving expression of the high literary culture to which the progressive Birmingham businessmen of the Chamberlain era aspired' – was retained in a new building.[98]

The replacement Central Library, designed by the John Madin Design Group, built in 1969–74 and once the largest public library in Europe, was itself proposed for demolition in 2001 and remains threatened at the time of writing, which suggests the decisions taken in the Birmingham of the 1960s were not altogether well considered.

The ASSIZE COURTS in MANCHESTER was the work that brought Alfred Waterhouse to national fame. He had won a competition for the new building in 1858, soon after the Prime Minister, Lord Palmerston, rejected Gilbert Scott's Gothic design for the new government offices in Whitehall. Not long after this intelligent essay in modern, colourful secular Gothic had been completed in 1865, Charles Eastlake wrote in his *History of the Gothic Revival* that,

> Time has shown that Mr. Waterhouse's plan for the Assize Courts is admirably adapted for its purpose; and, with regard to the artistic merit of the work, it will be time enough to criticise

Manchester Assize
Courts in c.1900, from a
postcard and in ruins after the
Second World War (along with
the campanile of Strangeways
Gaol) photographed by
T. Baddeley in 1945.

when any better modern structure of its size and style has been raised in this country.[99]

The success of the building led to Waterhouse being commissioned to design Strangeways Gaol and the Stipendiary Magistrates' Court in Manchester. The Assize Courts were gutted by bombs in 1940; only the Judge's Lodgings and the façade to Great Ducie Street survived intact. But the building stood, however, as a noble Ruskinian Gothic ruin until cleared away in the late 1950s: surely the exterior could have been retained? (The sculpture by Thomas Woolner and carving by the O'Shea brothers was salvaged and is now in the city's new Crown Court.) The Magistrates Court was demolished as late as the 1990s, when Strangeways Gaol, which had survived the war, was altered and enlarged after the 1990 prison riot: there is no justice in architectural preservation.

◄ The fortified entrance
to Holloway Prison,
photographed by Herbert
Felton.

There was no mistaking the function of HOLLOWAY PRISON in north London. It looked like a castle, although its purpose was to keep people in, rather than out. The rubble-stone walls were battlemented and the entrance was a symmetrical, twin-towered castle with turrets and pseudo-machicolations, while the tall central tower was modelled on Caesar's Tower at Warwick Castle. Inside, the buildings were more utilitarian and the radiating wings built of brick, although the cell windows were placed within pointed arches.

Originally designed as the City House of Correction by the City of London's architect, J.B. Bunning, the prison was built in 1849–51, but only became exclusively a women's prison in 1903. By the mid-20th century, the Mediaeval imagery given by the Victorians to their new prisons was considered oppressive and reactionary although, in truth, the chief problem was

▲▶ The General Post Office West Range in St-Martin's-le-Grand photographed by Herbert Felton in the 1930s and the G.P.O. in Spring Gardens in Manchester photographed by Sanville in 1954.

overcrowding due to Britain's inexorably rising prison population. 'New Wave' prisons were built in the 1950s, but the only example of replacing a Victorian prison that was actually achieved was the rebuilding of Holloway.

Because of its social connotations, the Victorian Society felt unable to plead for the retention of Bunning's impressive architecture and old Holloway was demolished in stages after 1970 for a new women's prison, completed in 1983 to the design of Robert Matthew Johnson-Marshall & Partners. But are blank red brick and concrete walls in the manner of an out-of-town shopping centre and a low-key entrance any less intimidating than Bunning's castle? After all, battlements or no, the building remains a prison, with all that that implies. This obsession with imagery and denigrating Victorian buildings might well suggest that Britain's attitude to prison reform is essentially half-hearted.

Despite the enthusiasm for the Gothic, the Classical tradition carried on well into Victoria's reign and managed to achieve some distinguished expressions – particularly in the official sphere. For, unlike today, the Victorians believed that public institutions deserved a dignified, sober architecture. This was particularly true of the GENERAL POST OFFICE. Writing in 1914, when the Gothic was quite out of fashion and a monumental Classicism again in vogue, Albert Richardson argued that,

The culminating phase of monumental architecture extended to practically as recent a date as 1870; in truth it exists later in the form of a wonderful aftermath, a further growth, the products of which connect the main movement to the events which are taking place to-day. The school of design engendered by the leadership of Professor Cockerell inspired the evolution of such monumental structures as the series of post-offices designed for the Office of Works by their architect, James Williams. In this regard the building at the junction of St. Martin's-le-Grand with Newgate Street, the Old Savings Bank in Queen Victoria Street and the splendid pile at Manchester deserve the highest consideration.[100]

Sadly, these noble, carefully detailed buildings by the undeservedly obscure Williams have all disappeared. The General Post Office in Spring Gardens, MANCHESTER, which Pevsner called 'a tremendous *palazzaccio*, like a Ministry building in Rome', was replaced by a banal, eight-storey tower in the late 1960s and the GPO Savings Bank in Queen Victoria Street made way for Faraday House, the nine-storey stone telephone exchange built in 1932–33, which was immediately denounced for the damage it did to views of St Paul's Cathedral.

The building on the west side of St Martin's-le-Grand was part of a complex of buildings for the Post Office. Built in 1869–73, it faced the original Greek Revival building by Sir Robert Smirke, which disappeared in 1912 after being replaced by the surviving King Edward Buildings further west. Williams' immensely distinguished West Range, richly modelled with much Mannerist invention which indeed owed much to Cockerell, was demolished in 1967 to make way for the British Telecom Centre.

8: PUBLIC AND PRIVATE INSTITUTIONS

As well as the employment of different styles for different purposes, the 19th century saw the development of distinct building types to fulfil the many functions required by the Victorian city. Such buildings were erected as much by individual or communal effort as by the action of the increasingly important municipal authorities: not just town halls, but museums and art galleries, libraries and clubs, schools and colleges, hospitals and asylums, prisons and cemeteries in addition to railway stations, banks, commercial buildings, markets and places of worship. 'The people of the twentieth century,' wrote the historian Asa Briggs, 50 years ago,

> have had to wrestle with complex urban problems bequeathed by the Victorians – health, housing, education and traffic, for example: at the same time they are still relying on the vast accumulation of social capital which the Victorians raised, usually by voluntary or by municipal effort. Much of the effort went into church building but particularly in the last twenty-five years of Queen Victoria's reign there was a huge development of public offices, hospitals,

schools, sewage farms and water works. The Victorian phase in city development cannot be ignored even as a visible factor in the present. It obtrudes in every provincial city and in London itself, although it is now being destroyed in the name of 'progress', a cause which was used by the Victorians themselves to sanctify much of their own destruction.[101]

As this quotation implies, much of this positive legacy has been squandered, often to no great effect, and particular building types, such as schools, have proved to be particularly vulnerable. The Victorians laid great stress on the importance of education and eventually made it free and compulsory. Much thought went into the design of school buildings – particularly of the Board Schools constructed under the 1870 Education Act – but many have been thoughtlessly demolished merely because they are, by chronological definition, 'Victorian'.

◄◄ The entrance portico at the Royal Victoria Hospital at Netley near Southampton, photographed in 1966.

In some cities, such as Liverpool, the Board Schools have almost all been wiped out, despite the fact that such buildings are often eminently suitable for other purposes. The wholesale destruction of Board Schools and other historic school buildings was last encouraged by the current government's 'Building Schools for the Future' programme and the use of the Private Finance Initiative, which militates against refurbishment in favour of profitable new build.

In recent years, the Victorian Society has challenged this prodigal and destructive policy, arguing that old schools have generously sized rooms, allowing a 'loose fit' usage; that old schools are usually of robust construction allowing easy adaptation, while being low-maintenance – in contrast to many newer structures; and that they are often important landmarks and symbols for communities. The basis of the government's programme, it points out,

> is that there is a direct relationship between the standards of education and the architectural standard of school buildings. The Victorian Society agrees with this; we merely wish to point out that high standards of architectural design can be found in old school buildings as well as in new ones.[102]

Furthermore, the desire to replace old school buildings so often proclaimed by blinkered politicians can exacerbate the unhappy distinction in Britain between state and private education – after all, so many public schools are conspicuous for their substantial Victorian buildings, often designed by well-known architects.

In recent years, swimming pools have proved to be even more problematic than old school buildings. The Victorians were much concerned with public hygiene and health, and the 1846 Baths and Wash Houses Act in particular encouraged the building of public baths and swimming pools. The consequence is that today, more historic pools survive in Britain than in other countries, and while many such buildings were severely utilitarian, many more – particularly those built later in the 19th century – are enjoyable structures of considerable architectural and decorative quality. And one reason for their survival, as a recent book published by English Heritage argues, is that

> baths were built so robustly and using such high quality materials that – interludes of inadequate maintenance and under-funding notwithstanding – they have endured extremely well and in some cases much better than many of their modern counterparts. They are buildings for which, quite literally, local authorities, architects and engineers, builders and craftsmen, manufacturers and designers, and most importantly of all, the ratepayers of Britain have gone to great lengths to procure.[103]

Swimming pools are expensive to maintain while being, for obvious reasons, difficult to adapt to other uses. However, as Hana and Alastair Laing pointed out 30 years ago in the pioneering report by SAVE Britain's Heritage on the threat to the architecture of bathing,

> Most local authorities now seem to see public baths as an embarrassing legacy from the past. So, often needlessly, they have simply demolished fine examples of older baths, rather than trying to see how they might be preserved and adapted. They have given no thought to the example set by Michelangelo's conversion of the Baths of Diocletian in Rome into a church for the Carthusians. Unless similar imagination is applied to our public baths, we shall soon have nothing to remind us of one of the miss enlightened impulses of Victorian philanthropy, and we shall have lost a whole category of proud civic architecture'.[104]

Unfortunately, many Victorian and Edwardian pools have been, and continue to be closed and disposed of by the local authorities that run them, despite the government's much-vaunted concern with obesity and poor public health, and with encouraging exercise and sport. Often despite local protest, fine examples of Victorian and Edwardian public baths architecture have been demolished, sometimes to be replaced by modern swimming pools, but often not. At the time of writing, out of over 50 listed pool buildings still standing, only 14 remain in use for the purpose for which they were designed.

In contrast, a high proportion of Victorian hospital buildings survive in use although by the nature of their function, the original buildings have usually been altered and extended, often in a crudely utilitarian manner. It may also be true to say that, as many of them were former workhouses, their architecture was, in general, not of the best and most sympathetic kind. But the Victorian building type which has proved to be the most misunderstood and vulnerable to the point of extinction is surely the lunatic asylum. Owing, in part, to sheer ignorance combined with memories of how the 18th century treated the insane, it has too often been assumed that these large buildings, set remotely in extensive grounds, were cruel and oppressive institutions – an opinion encouraged by changing theories and fashions about the best treatment of mental illness. In fact, as Sarah Rutherford, historian of the Victorian asylum points out, 'they were constructed as benevolent and compassionate faculties for vulnerable people'. Furthermore, the landscaped and cultivated grounds by which they were surrounded embodied a vision for healing, which was based on the country house in its estate.

> Victorian asylums sheltered and supported people with mental illness and learning difficulties. Each had its own community, based on a great building, park and garden, and was intended to be therapeutic and to help cure the patients.[105]

A huge number of large new asylums were built during Queen Victoria's reign. Between 1859 and 1909 the population of England and Wales doubled while the number of publicly-funded asylums increased five-fold, so that, by 1914, there were over 100,000 patients in 102 asylums. These buildings were often imposing and architecturally pretentious, with several designed by notable architects. Since the 1960s, however, with better medication and other treatments combined with the promotion of what has been euphemistically called 'care in the community' rather than long-term residence in institutions, almost all Victorian asylums were closed by the 1990s.

'Not since the Beeching Axe fell on the railways has so large a slice of the nation's architectural heritage been made so precipitately redundant,' announced Marcus Binney in 1995, in a report on the problem issued by SAVE Britain's Heritage.

> By the year 2000, 98 out of a total 121 large mental hospitals (open in 1986) will have closed. At stake, are a series of the largest, most remarkable and little known public buildings in England built at great expense and set in superb landscape grounds which are often now in the full splendour of maturity. The quality of these buildings is the greater as so many were the subject of architectural competitions.[106]

The closure of these institutions may or may not be a good thing in social terms, but what has also taken place in recent decades is a ruthless and cynical exercise in asset-stripping by the government. In most cases the sites seemed ripe for development and have been sold by the National Health Service, with the result that solid, adaptable and sometimes distinguished buildings were demolished or mutilated while the asylum grounds have been covered by housing estates. Victorian mental asylums were eminently suitable for conversion into housing but, as SAVE Britain's Heritage complained,

> too many are at the mercy of agents and planning consultants who, in flagrant disregard of the latest government guidelines, often insist that the buildings must be demolished and the sites broken up, brushing off approaches from experienced developers and architects with imaginative and viable proposals of alternative use which will be of great benefit in local communities.

Dozens of these fine buildings have been demolished and their grounds despoiled.

▶ A 19th photograph of the Carlton Club in Pall Mall.

The CARLTON CLUB was one of several grand club-houses built in Pall Mall during the 19th century. Just as it was High Tory in opposition to the Whig politics of the Reform Club, so its ebullient, sculptural Classicism was intended as an answer to the restrained palazzo style used by Barry next door. Founded in 1832, the Carlton was the first of the political clubs, but its original home – designed by Sir Robert Smirke, architect of the British Museum – was soon thought to be too small.

In 1844 it was decided to build something grander and twice as big. A muddled competition resulted in Smirke's younger brother Sydney, together with George Basevi, being selected as joint architects. Basevi fell off the west tower of Ely Cathedral in 1845, leaving 'little Syd' in sole charge of this important commission. Already he had designed the Conservative and Oxford & Cambridge Clubs and now chose to use a rich, colourful Renaissance manner inspired by 17th-century Venice, in particular by Sansovino's Library of St Mark. The principal entablature was elaborately decorated and there was sculpture framing the first-floor arched windows – as in Venice. Further richness was achieved by the pioneering use in London of polished columns of pink and green granite.

One commentator thought the design 'marks the triumph of Italianism over Greekism'[107] and the building, completed in 1854, heralded the opulence of High Victorian Classicism. Unfortunately, in addition to Aberdeen and Peterhead granite, Smirke used Caen stone on the exterior of the club, but this rapidly failed and the details began to crumble (the same problem as with Edward Blore's front to Buckingham Palace). In 1923, Sir Reginald Blomfield was asked to reface the building. Typically, he rejected Smirke's polychromy in favour of sober Portland stone. Equally typically, just as Herbert Baker could not resist improving Taylor's and Soane's work when he rebuilt the Bank of England that same decade, so Blomfield changed Smirke's design. Despite the voluble opposition of Lord Curzon, this was carried out. However, Smirke's palatial interior, with rooms arranged around a central cortile, survived until 1940 when the building was bombed and gutted. The shell lingered for a while, eventually being replaced by the distinguished abstracted Classical façades of No.100 Pall Mall by Donald McMorran. For once, a fine Victorian building was replaced by a really good, 20th-century one.

◀ The Clothworkers' Hall tucked away off Mincing Lane, a photograph taken from *Lost London* by Hermione Hobhouse (1971) as the original is no longer available.

The CLOTHWORKERS' HALL in Mincing Lane was one of several City of London livery companies' premises rebuilt in Victoria's reign. The building, a strongly modelled but disciplined design in the Victorian Cinquecento manner, was the work of Samuel Angell, who had been surveyor to the Clothworkers' Company since 1824. A pupil of Thomas Hardwick, he had earlier made archaeological discoveries at Greek temples at Selinus in Sicily. Designed in 1856, the new hall was opened by Prince Albert in 1860. However, this handsome, accomplished building was destroyed by bombs in 1940; the present, replacement Clothworkers' Hall is housed in a large Neo-Georgian block of offices.

BRADFORD'S MECHANICS INSTITUTE was a fine example of one of the voluntary institutions that did so much to improve Victorian cities and generate a sense of civic pride. 'The Mechanics Institutes were nineteenth-century inventions, products of the age of improvement,' Asa Briggs has written.[108] And another historian, Tristram Hunt, has observed that,

> The urban elites of the 19th century believed passionately in joining associations and founding clubs. Friendly societies, voluntary societies and fraternities made up the rich tapestry of Victorian civic life. By 1850, there were more than 700 mechanics' institutes, literary institutes, athenaeums and mutual improvement societies commanding a combined membership of more than 120,000 people in Yorkshire and Lancashire alone.[109]

Bradford's Mechanics' Institute was founded in 1825 to encourage the improvement of the rapidly expanding town's working class. Its library was established seven years later and was very important for adult education. It was in the Institute's earlier, Greek Revival home (itself now demolished) that John Ruskin gave his lecture on the social morality of architecture that was subsequently published as 'The Crown of Wild Olive'.

A new home for the Institute was built in Bridge Street, close to the Town Hall, in 1871. It was designed in a Venetian Renaissance style by the firm of Andrews & Pepper, architects of the magnificent (and surviving) Manningham Mill. A century later, Bradford's notion of civic pride was to eliminate as much as possible of the city's Victorian past (see pages 35 and 77). Shortly after its centenary was celebrated in 1971, the grimy, but still active home of the Mechanics' Institute was demolished and in 1974, its site was cleared to make an open space now part of Centenary Square. At least the library was not dispersed or destroyed, but has been housed elsewhere.

The ROYAL ARCHITECTURAL MUSEUM in Westminster had a chequered and unfortunate history. It was a product of the Gothic Revival. In 1851, the year of the Great Exhibition, a group of architects – notably George Gilbert Scott – urged the purchase of the collection of Mediaeval casts and architectural fragments assembled by Lewis Cottingham so that it could be expanded as a national museum of architecture for the use of carvers and sculptors working on new buildings and become a school of art for art workmen. With the support of Prince Albert, this idea was realised.

The first home of the Architectural Museum was in a wharf by the Thames in Cannon Row, but financial problems and shortage of space resulted in the collection being transferred to the South Kensington Museum a few years later. This association was unhappy and money was raised to move the collection of casts to purpose-built premises in Tufton Street. The building which opened in 1869 had been designed by Joseph Clarke together with Ewan Christian, architect to the Ecclesiastical Commissioners. Its severe brick façade was French Gothic in style but, inevitably, was enriched with sculpture. For a time the museum flourished, but with the waning of the Gothic Revival it soon began to struggle. In 1893, the building was enlarged to house the Westminster School of Art.

A decade later the whole building and its contents was offered as a free gift to the Architectural Association, which was seeking larger premises. In 1903–04, the building was altered and adapted by Leonard Stokes, and subsequently the

▲▶ The collection of the Royal Architectural Museum in its purpose-built home in 1872–73 and the building in Tufton Street, Westminster, in 1916 after it had been taken over by the Architectural Association.

original façade was spoiled and some sculpture removed. But the move to Tufton Street was soon regretted and in 1916, the Architectural Association moved to Bedford Square while the collection of casts was sent back to South Kensington, where some of them may be found in the Cast Courts of the Victoria & Albert Museum. The curious, ill-fated building in Tufton Street was bought by the National Lending Library For The Blind and lingered on until about 1935.

The INSTITUTE OF THE FINE ARTS building in GLASGOW was both a notably fine and enjoyable art gallery and the first important independent work by one of the city's greatest architects. The Institute was founded in 1861 to have public exhibitions of the work of Glasgow's modern artists. It was so successful that it was decided to build its own premises on a site in Sauchiehall Street. A competition held in 1878 was won by the local architect John Burnet. In fact, the design was made by his son, the future Sir John James Burnet, who had recently returned from studying at the Ecole des Beaux-Arts in Paris and was his father's junior partner. The building was finished in time to house the Institute's annual exhibition in 1879 and the younger Burnet regarded it as the first he could call his own. In the design, he aimed 'to combine Greek with modern French Renaissance'[110] and he drew upon the architectural tradition established in Glasgow by Alexander 'Greek' Thomson.

▶ The Institute of the Fine Arts in Sauchiehall Street, Glasgow, photographed by T. & R. Annan in 1955 after it had become part of a department store.

The Chiswick School of Art, photographed by Bedford Lemere in 1881.

The façade in Sauchiehall Street was a brilliant essay in interpenetrating orders above a severe Thomsonian basement with a central and rather Parisian arched entrance. At high level, the areas of windowless wall required by an art gallery were relieved by a Parthenon-like frieze by John and William Mossman, the accomplished Glasgow sculptors. The interior was more purely Grecian. Unfortunately, in 1902, the Institute decided to revert to hiring the nearby McLellan Galleries for

The School Board of London offices in Temple Place overlooking Victoria Embankment Gardens soon after completion in 1874.

its exhibitions and the building was sold to Messrs Pettigrew & Stephens. It was used by the department store until 1967, when the upper part was demolished. The residue was destroyed in 1973–74 when the handsome Pettigrew & Stephens building, designed by Honeyman & Keppie and detailed by C.R. Mackintosh, together with its neighbour, the premises of Messrs Copeland & Lye, were cleared and replaced by the peculiarly nasty brick-faced shopping centre and car park known as the Sauchiehall Centre.

The CHISWICK SCHOOL OF ART was one of the few public buildings to grace the new artistic London suburb of Bedford Park. Built in Bath Road, it was designed in 1881 by Maurice B. Adams in the 'Queen Anne' style that Norman Shaw had introduced to give the suburb its distinctive, progressive character. Shaw, however, was not altogether impressed with the design and amended it before it was carried out. The five Dutch gables, the Baroque doorway in rubbed red-brick and the Oriel windows were all typical of the style, but the composition, although charming, somehow lacked the suavity and subtlety of Shaw.

Later part of the Chiswick Polytechnic, the School of Art building was hit by a flying bomb towards the end of the Second World War and completely demolished.

The Education Act of 1870 introduced by W.E. Forster established elected school boards all over Britain charged with providing sufficient elementary school accommodation. School attendance became compulsory in 1880, by which date many new schools had been built, and free in 1891. In 1872, the SCHOOL BOARD OF LONDON decided to erect offices for itself overlooking the new Victoria Embankment. A limited competition was won by G.F. Bodley and his partner, Thomas Garner, architects best known for churches but for this commission they eschewed Gothic and adopted a version of the progressive 'Queen Anne' style being used by other architects for the new Board Schools as well as houses.

Built of red brick and stone with mullioned and transomed windows and elaborate dormer gables, it was more French, or reminiscent of Antwerp, than English. Bodley wrote that

The Bonner Street School in Bethnal Green in the 1880s before it was enlarged and as it looked in 2005 shortly before demolition.

the style adopted is a free form of Classic or Renaissance. The style allows of the freedom and pliability characteristic of Gothic, and has the advantage of giving ample window space and square headed windows instead of pointed ones.[111]

Completed in 1874, the building was furnished by the firm of Watts & Co, newly founded by Bodley, Garner and G.G. Scott junior. But it was soon found to be too small and in the early 1890s was almost tripled in size by Colonel Robert Edis, who doubled up Bodley's elevation and added wings and a central tower. The responsibilities of the London School Board were transferred to the London County Council in 1904, and the building was demolished in 1929 to be replaced by Herbert Baker's Electra House, which has itself since been demolished.

The new schools commissioned by the London School Board soon became prominent and influential landmarks. Tall buildings of brick, with Flemish gables and big windows, they were tangible advertisements for the new 'Queen Anne' style. 'Lighthouses, my boy! Beacons of the future!' Sir Arthur Conan Doyle had Sherlock Holmes say to Dr Watson as they saw such schools rising above the rooftops from a train near Clapham Junction; 'Capsules, with hundreds of bright little seeds in each, out of which will spring the wiser, better England of the future'.[112]

Many of the early schools were designed by Edward Robert Robson, the School Board's chief architect and sometime partner of J.J. Stevenson: one such was the BONNER STREET SCHOOL in Bethnal Green. Built in 1876, on a corner site and much enlarged in the same style in 1914, it remained in school use for a century and a quarter, having survived both the Second World War and subsequent slum-clearance schemes, and could easily have continued to serve the local community. However, Tower Hamlets Council decided to rebuild the school under the government's 'Building Schools for the Future' programme.

A new school was built on a site that had once been a community garden. The contractor doing the work under the Private Finance Initiative claimed it was too expensive to refurbish the old Board School, which could have been sold for conversion into flats. Instead it was decided to demolish it to create playground space. The Victorian Society asked for the building to be listed and a petition for it to be retained was signed by teachers and local residents but after much controversy this much-loved local landmark was demolished in 2006.

Not all the early London Board Schools were designed in the progressive 'Queen Anne' style. In 1873–74, Robson built a school in WINSTANLEY ROAD on an awkward site in Battersea, close to Clapham Junction Station, in an individual manner in brick, which combined large sash windows with Gothic elements. A projecting staircase tower rose to a sort of open belfry, the

main south-facing elevation enhanced by a sculptured panel by Spencer Stanhope representing 'Knowledge strangling Ignorance'.

Robson was clearly pleased with the design as he published it in his 1874 book on *School Architecture*, noting that it 'possesses a more castellated character than perhaps any other among the Board schools'. The building was later extended and in 1901–02, it was remodelled by T.J. Bailey, but was demolished in 1939. Owing to the outbreak of the Second World War, the new school intended to replace it was never built.

Board Schools in other English cities continue to fall victim to prodigal and wasteful policies by both central government and local authorities. In MANCHESTER, the first generation of Board schools were Gothic in style. All have now gone, including the DUCIE AVENUE SCHOOL, which was built in 1880–82 to the designs of J.W. Beaumont, later the architect of the Whitworth Art Gallery in Manchester. The school was closed in the 1970s and the original building, hidden by later extensions, stood derelict until it was demolished in 2009.

In LIVERPOOL, almost every one of the city's Board Schools has been demolished in recent years. Buildings once regarded as exemplifying the city's educational achievements in the later 19th century were regarded as dispensable by the early 21st century. Some fell victim to comprehensive redevelopment schemes; more perished after they were closed following reform of Liverpool's much-criticised education system – as if innocent buildings were to blame for low standards and institutional incompetence.

The Victorian Society and local groups pressed for the spot listing of good examples of the city's historic school buildings, but in vain. The TIBER STREET COUNTY PRIMARY SCHOOL,

built in 1904, was a good and unusual example, built of brick and terra-cotta. It was closed in 1999 and demolished soon afterwards.

BARNWELL ABBEY NATIONAL SCHOOL in CAMBRIDGE was one of the many church schools promoted by the National Society, founded in 1811. Built in 1858–59, in River Lane to the east of the city centre, it was the work of Richard Reynolds Rowe, architect of the Corn Exchange, who, with his penchant for polychromatic brickwork and chunky detail, can be regarded as Cambridge's own 'rogue' architect.

The Barnwell Abbey School, for girls and infants, was Gothic in style and dominated by a tall turret, intended both for bells and ventilation, which changed in plan from square to octagon to circle before terminating in a conical roof. The school was used by the New Street Men's Bible Class by the 1930s, later renamed Mansfield Hall. After the Second World War, the turret lost its tiled hat and the whole building was demolished in 1973 as part of the City Council's redevelopment of the area.

▲ Mansfield Hall, the former Barnwell Abbey National School in Cambridge, as it looked in 1938.

The DURNFORD STREET ELEMENTARY SCHOOL was built in 1908-10 and was one of two schools in MIDDLETON, Lancashire, designed by the partnership of Edgar Wood and James Henry Sellers, who were responsible for some of the most intriguing and progressive buildings erected in England before the Great War. Wood was responsible for the Christian Science church in Manchester, a work comparable with celebrated Art Nouveau and Jugendstil buildings on the Continent. The Middleton schools, however, seem to have been largely the work of Sellers, who introduced an austere cubic aesthetic, which anticipates the Art Deco of the 1920s.

Like the contemporary house at Stafford

◀ The Durnford Street Elementary School in Middleton, Lancashire, in c.1912.

The entrance front and the ladies' pool at the Latchmere Road Baths in Battersea, photographed in the 1970s.

called 'Upmeads', the schools were designed in a sort of abstracted Tudor manner, with flat roofs of reinforced concrete. Both Middleton schools had cavity walls of brick supporting concrete floors and roofs. Pevsner, in 1969, recognised their importance, noting, 'They have certain C17 and C18 features, but their planning is fresh and convincing, and their general appearance is strikingly cubic. Here, by experiment, two Lancashire architects of no great renown got as near to anyone in England to the most progressive European and American work of 1900–14'.

Earlier, in 1942, in an essay lamenting the failure of such experiments to evolve into a convincing modern architecture in Britain, Pevsner praised 'such novel and adventurous buildings as the Elm Street and Durnford Street Schools at Middleton, Manchester, with motifs that stand just midway between Townsend's Art Nouveau and the Western Avenue style' [i.e., Deco].[113]

Unfortunately, the Durnford Street School fell victim to the structural defects associated with many pioneering reinforced concrete buildings. There were problems with the asphalt-covered flat roof, which leaked. Furthermore, the special thin red facing bricks turned out to have been poorly fired and began to disintegrate. The school closed in 1992 and was finally demolished in 2002 after a

Henry Hare's handsome façade for the Pitfield Street Baths in Shoreditch soon after completion.

decade of neglect and vandalism despite being listed at Grade II, and a campaign for its repair and reuse mounted by Wood's and Sellers' biographer John Archer and the Victorian Society.

Among institutional buildings serving a public need, swimming pools have proved as vulnerable and expendable as schools in recent years – perhaps more so as they are expensive to build and maintain, and not so easily converted to alternative uses. Many Victorian public baths, in which a swimming pool was combined with bathing and washhouse facilities, were utilitarian buildings, but some, often when combined with a library or other such institution, were of considerable architectural pretension. Only a few representative examples can be illustrated here.

The LATCHMERE ROAD BATHS in BATTERSEA in London was built in 1889. With its handsome Jacobean façade, it was designed by Rowland Plumbe, a prolific architect of institutional buildings in London, with Horace T. Bonner and Charles Jones. As with many swimming pools, the proposal to close and replace the swimming pool by the London Borough of Wandsworth provoked a local protest campaign, but the building was nevertheless demolished in 1981. Unlike Plumbe's building, its replacement – which could equally well be a warehouse – is of no architectural merit and makes no positive contribution to the urban topography.

The PITFIELD STREET BATHS & WASHHOUSES in east London were built by the Shoreditch Vestry

and opened in 1899. The Vestry had decided that public baths and a library should be combined in one building to form part of a civic centre and a competition held in 1895 was won by Henry T. Hare, the accomplished architect of the Municipal Buildings in Oxford, Westminster College at Cambridge and University College at Bangor in Wales.

The handsome elevations he designed for Shoreditch were in a free Tudor Renaissance style in red brick and stone, tinged with Art Nouveau. The Passmore Edwards Library was all Hare's own work, but his plans for the interior were considered less successful and for the public baths the firm of Henry Spalding & Alfred W.S. Cross, experts in swimming pool design, were brought in as joint architects. The baths were remarkable, not least for being the first to be powered by electricity generated by a 'dust destructor' or refuse incinerator. The building contained two pools and 76 slipper baths, and was much used and valued at a time when most houses did not contain a bath.

Both baths and library were damaged during the Second World War. The baths reopened in 1951, but 10 years later they were closed by the local authority and the site leased to National Car Parks in 1962 on condition that the buildings were demolished. Hare's library survives.

The long-lost BRILL'S BATHS in BRIGHTON were an architectural phenomenon as well as a curiosity. Their history is complicated. They

succeeded a bathhouse opened in 'Pool Valley' in Brighton, in 1769, by Dr John Awsiter. Close by, in Grand Junction Road, Abraham Lamprell opened the town's first communal swimming bath in 1823, known, because of its circular shape, as 'the bunion'.

His nephew, Charles Brill, inherited the concern and built a new ladies' bath in the Gothic style on the site of Awsiter's in 1861. A few years later, he decided to rebuild his baths, creating a 65ft diameter circular pool – the largest in Europe at the time – filled with 80,000 gallons of seawater from Hove, as Brighton water was considered too polluted. To design the building containing it, as well as the associated baths, reading room and billiard room, Brill went not to a local architect, but a national figure: George Gilbert Scott, who had family connections in Brighton.

In 1866, Scott designed red brick buildings in his secular Gothic manner, with an intriguing irregular rhythm of windows. He also again showed how comfortable he was with iron structures by raising an iron and glass top-lit dome above the Gothic arcading and spectators' gallery that surrounded the circular pool. The new baths opened in 1869. But the popularity of such baths declined in the following century and Brill's Baths were demolished in 1929 to be replaced by the Savoy Cinema.

Nikolaus Pevsner described the ROYAL VICTORIA HOSPITAL at NETLEY in Hampshire as 'A monster of a building'. It certainly was enormous. Soon after the Crimean War had exposed the incompetence of the British military establishment and Florence Nightingale's efforts at Scutari revealed to a wider public the sufferings and disgraceful mortality of soldiers being treated out there, it was proposed to build one large new military hospital back in Britain. A site was found next to Southampton Water, close to the ruins of Netley Abbey, so that sick and wounded soldiers could arrive by sea as well as by railway. Queen Victoria, who had taken a close interest in the subject, laid the foundation stone in 1856.

The project soon became controversial, however, because the planning took little heed of Miss Nightingale's recommendations for new hospitals and she became a severe critic of the design. Work on its massive, solid construction went remorselessly ahead, however, and the 1,424ft long building, vaguely in the manner of Wren and topped with domes and towers, opened its doors to military patients in 1863. Sir Charles Barry may have been approached to provide plans but in the event the hospital was designed by a military surveyor. In his evocative biography of the building, Philip Hoare describes how,

◄ ▼ The Royal Victoria
Hospital at Netley in 1966
shortly before demolition
began and a photograph from
Lady Hornby's album showing
the huge building in c.1868
with the 1864 memorial
to members of the Army
Medical Department who
died in the Crimean War in the
foreground.

Everything about the place was monumental. Its architecture aspired to eighteenth-century rationality, yet it spoke of nineteenth-century imperialism. Somehow the sense of proportion had been subtly overbalanced, as though designed by a team of architects whom no one had told to stop, its creators having suffered a fit of megalomania. But the building was also the product of bureaucracy, dwarfing the mere human like some enormous town hall conceived by committee. From a dark interior of the War Office, orders had been issued to E.O. Mennie, Surveyor of the Royal Engineer Department, and his army of assistants in Pall Mall, an architectural sweatshop producing sheet after sheet of plans, measurements and specifications. This was a building under royal patronage, created by the richest and most powerful nation on earth, and nothing was to be spared in realising its imperial vision.[114]

Built of the best brickwork and Portland stone, it lasted for just over a century. For a time the home of the Army Medical School, filled with shell-shocked casualties and prisoners of war during the First World War and used by the United States Army in the Second, the neglected building ceased to be a hospital in 1956 – when General Sir George Erskine claimed it was a 'shocker' and should be pulled down and used as hard core for roads.

For a few years it stood empty and vandalised. It now seems hard to believe that no new use could have been found for so solid a structure. As Pevsner

▲▶ The Buckinghamshire County Lunatic Asylum at Stone near Aylesbury in 1897 photographed by Frith & Co.

pointed out, 'The wings would each make reasonable major buildings in themselves, and are quite impressively composed'.[115] Demolition began in 1966 and only the centrally placed Royal Chapel, with its domed tower, was allowed to survive.

The BUCKINGHAMSHIRE COUNTY LUNATIC ASYLUM was built in 1850–53 at STONE, near Aylesbury, on a fine site overlooking the Chilterns. The red brick buildings in a restrained Italianate Classical style were designed by Thomas Henry Wyatt and David Brandon, both notable architects, who had won a competition held in 1849. Later additions to the asylum were made by Brandon alone, including the detached flint-faced chapel of 1868–69. The Oxford Regional Health Authority decided to close what was by now called St John's Hospital in 1983 and this was done in 1991. Three years later, Marcus Binney visited the site:

> Here was a very large cottage style asylum – consisting of numerous three-sided courtyards of two storey accommodation and simply begging to be divided into two storey houses. Better still – the main south-facing range had for its whole length a magnificent panorama over the Vale of Aylesbury. Not a house, not an 'Atcost' barn was to be seen amidst the patchwork of fields, woods and hedges. I was taken there by a local architect [Eric Throssel] who on his own

initiative had drawn up plans showing how it could become a model village. We were too late. Demolition was already under way.[116]

English Heritage declined to recommend the buildings for listing and the local council was keen to build a by-pass around Stone and build houses and businesses on the surrounding land. Two hundred and fifty houses now cover the grounds. This is but one of many examples of well designed, solidly built Victorian asylums with great potential, foolishly thrown away because of narrow, short-term thinking.

The SAILORS' HOME in LIVERPOOL was one of the most remarkable of the many magnificent buildings wilfully squandered in that most exasperating city since the Second World War. Designed by John Cunningham, it stood, like a tall Elizabethan prodigy house, right behind John Foster's magnificent Custom House in Canning Place, close to the Mersey and the docks. The foundation stone was laid by Prince Albert in 1846 and this palatial lodging house opened its doors two years later. (although the interior had to be rebuilt after a fire in 1860).

Built by subscription from merchants and shipowners, the Sailors' Home was a philanthropic institution offering good, clean and reasonably priced accommodation to sailors who might

▲▶ The Sailors' Home in Liverpool: the grand turreted exterior and the internal galleried court photographed in 1969.

otherwise be tempted by the grog shops, disreputable lodging houses and worse. Inside this stone castle, rooms were arranged around a tapering top-lit inner courtyard surrounded by cast-iron balconies, which Pevsner found 'an amazing sight'. 'If to some the interior of the Home appears somewhat like a prison,' wrote Quentin Hughes in 1964,

> this was not Cunningham's concept. He modelled it on ship's quarters with cabins ranged around five stories of galleries in the internal rhomboidal court. The columns and balustrades of the galleries are powerfully moulded in cast iron using nautical themes like turned rope, twisted dolphins, and mermaids.[117]

This decorative treatment of the ironwork brings Bunning's contemporary Coal Exchange to mind (see page 72); indeed, these two composite structures were considered together as 'outlaw buildings' by Goodhart-Rendel in his 1959 lecture on choosing which Victorian buildings deserved protection. They were, he thought,

> being quintessentially Victorian are so obviously conservanda that they cannot be passed without mention. I do not rate highly the aesthetic value of either, but their historical and associational value is intense. After all, neither is as ugly as Stonehenge.[118]

The Sailors' Home avoided the bombs which gutted the Custom House in the Second World War and, unlike Foster's masterpiece which Liverpool Corporation chose to destroy rather than restore, it survived another quarter-century. But the authorities chose to run the building down rather than bring the standard of accommodation up to modern standards. The Sailors' Home closed its doors in 1969 and was demolished four years later. For three decades the site remained empty and is now occupied by a shopping centre.

9: DOMESTIC ARCHITECTURE, URBAN AND SUBURBAN

Every type of dwelling, whether grand or humble, urban, suburban or rural, can be found in the wide range of Victorian architecture, as can every style: Italianate Classical and Greek, Tudor and Gothic, eclectic 'Queen Anne', rustic 'Old English' vernacular and interesting experiments in trying to find a new style for the times. Certain well-established building types, such as the aristocratic town mansion and the terraced house, continued to be built right through the 19th century, but with their impatience with Georgian repetition and blandness, these were invigorated with ebullience in different styles. There were also new domestic building types which the Victorians made their own, notably the suburban villa and the vicarage, both of which – in their asymmetrical picturesqueness – owed much to the examples created by the great Pugin. There was also the innovation of the artist's studio-house, which emerged in the middle of Victoria's reign, particularly in Hampstead and Chelsea.

Some of these buildings were among the most important and influential of their time, but many have gone. Several of the grand 'private palaces' in London went between the world wars – along with their Georgian predecessors – as, in the radically changed post-war conditions, their sites were sold for profitable replacement by blocks of flats. The usual complaint of the 20th century against the houses of the 19th was that they were too large, too unmanageable and too expensive to maintain and heat, especially without servants. Changes in technology, as well as in ways of living, meant that buildings once perfectly designed for a particular style of life and income soon became inconvenient. Yet many of these buildings could have survived, had they been subdivided or used for other purposes, and their loss has diminished the quality and interest of our city and suburban streets.

DORCHESTER HOUSE in Park Lane was built in Victoria's reign but it was in the tradition of Grosvenor House, Chesterfield House and the other earlier aristocratic townhouses, which stood nearby in Mayfair. As far as Beresford Chancellor, author of a study of *The Private Palaces of London*, was concerned, 'Of all the great houses in

◄◄ The grand staircase hall in Dorchester House, Park Lane, photographed by Bedford Lemere for Beresford Chancellor's 1908 book, The Private Palaces of London.

▶ The exterior of Dorchester House in Park Lane in an early 20th century photograph.

Park Lane, none equal – none, indeed, approach in splendour – Dorchester House, which may, I think, without hyperbole, be considered the finest private dwelling in London, as well as London's most graceful and beautiful attempt at modern domestic architecture'.[119]

Solidly and magnificently constructed of the finest materials, it was built by the millionaire collector Robert Stayner Holford, both for entertaining and to house his renowned collection of paintings. Holford's architect was Lewis Vulliamy, who designed this Italianate palace in 1848–49. The principal rooms were not completed until 1860, but the house was never entirely finished because the paintings in the state dining room commissioned from Alfred Stevens remained unexecuted at the artist's death in 1875.

Holford died in 1892; for a time his palace was used by the Shah of Persia, later it became the residence of the United States Ambassador. But after Holford's son died in 1926, his collection was sold and Dorchester House put on the market. It could have been saved: there was a most appropriate proposal that it become the Italian Embassy, while Lady Beecham campaigned for it to be a centre for opera and Shakespeare but the site was acquired by the Gordon Hotels Company and the house demolished in 1929 to be replaced by the Dorchester Hotel. The house sale held that year revealed how times had changed; as *The Times* reported,

> men were grudgingly bidding in units for splendours designed in pride and bought for lavish hundreds . . .; the Grand Marble Staircase, trodden by feet of princes, lit by and lighting up of old the bright eyes of beauty, fell at £273. It had cost £30,000. Dorchester House is dead; and it is better so. The present age is not attuned to it.[120]

At least the great chimneypieces carved by Alfred Stevens found their way into museums in London and Liverpool.

MONTAGU HOUSE in WHITEHALL was one of the last and largest aristocratic houses to be built in London. If not as distinguished architecturally as Dorchester House, it was expensive and magnificently constructed. Montagu House stood on an historic site once occupied by Whitehall Palace. The existing Georgian house on the site was rebuilt in 1858–64 by the 5th Duke of Buccleuch. His architect was also Scottish, the doyen of early 19th-century country house

◄ The Whitehall front of
Montagu House in 1929.

planners, William Burn, who designed a very large stone mansion with high pavilion roofs in the French Renaissance style. One front faced Whitehall while another symmetrical elevation overlooked the gardens, which stretched down to the Thames until the Victoria Embankment was constructed shortly afterwards.

The Crown repossessed the lease in 1917 and the Grand Rooms then used by the Ministry of Trade and it was later occupied by the Ministry of Labour. By then it was scheduled for demolition to make way for the large block of government offices on the east side of Whitehall first proposed before the Great War. This project eventually became the long block designed by Vincent Harris for the Board of Trade and Air Ministry, which was built in phases between 1939 and 1959. Montagu House managed to survive the Second World War, but was demolished a few years later.

By the end of the century, it was not the old aristocracy but a new plutocracy, often men who had made their fortunes in South Africa, building ostentatious mansions in the West End of London. A good example was ALDFORD HOUSE in Park Lane. The site was leased in 1893 by the South African diamond tycoon Alfred Beit, but various conditions were imposed by the Duke of Westminster, notably a restriction on height to protect the outlook from the houses in Park Street behind. The building that was completed in 1896 was not wholly satisfactory. Outside was a rather squat Arts & Crafts interpretation of Jacobean in Portland stone. The interior was intended to be panelled as in a country house but this was not to Beit's taste and in the event the rooms were done in the French manner conventionally favoured by the contemporary nouveau riche. All this was a pity as the architects were good: Balfour & Turner; that is, Col. Eustace Balfour, brother of the future Prime Minister, and Hugh Thackeray Turner, an associate of William Morris, whose heart lay in rural Surrey.

As David Pearce commented, 'Architects wedded to the Arts and Crafts movement and to the principles of William Morris's Society for the Protection of Ancient Buildings should have had no business building fin de siècle palaces on Park Lane for South African millionaires'.[121] But they did because the well-connected Balfour also acted as surveyor to the Grosvenor Estate.

Alford House had a short life. Beit died in 1906, later occupants changed the interior and it was demolished in 1931 as the Grosvenor Estate

▶ Alford House in Park Lane
in c.1926.

by then wanted something more substantial and profitable on the site.

Further south in Park Lane, an unusual and much smaller house had a rather longer life. NO. 23, PARK LANE, was Gothic, in marked contrast

▼ Houses in Park Lane including Gothic No.23 designed by W.B. Moffatt, all cleared for the Hilton Hotel in 1960.

to its terraced neighbours. Completed in 1848 for Charles Russell, its tall, thin elevation had a two-storey projecting oriel window rising above a single buttress. This imaginative and pioneering urban essay in Perpendicular Gothic owed much to Pugin and its architect was William Bonython Moffatt, who is best known as the early partner of George Gilbert Scott.

Moffatt had talent, but his career was sad. Dangerously involved in speculation during the Railway Mania of the 1840s – which is why Mrs Scott terminated the partnership with her husband in 1846 – he later took to drink, was imprisoned for debt and ended up in Australia. Along with its neighbours, this interesting house was cleared in 1960 to make way for the Hilton Hotel.

THE RED HOUSE in BAYSWATER was a most influential terraced house designed by John James Stevenson, the Glasgow architect who had come south and embraced the new domestic 'Queen Anne' style. Built in 1871–73, of London stock brick with red brick dressings, with its projecting bay rising through three floors, its prominent dormer windows with Flemish gables, its niches, shutters and 17th-century 'Queen Anne' detail, it was in marked contrast to the conventional stucco-fronted Victorian terraced

▲▶ The entrance to the Red House and the house flanked by its neighbours in the Bayswater Road, photographed by Sydney Newbery in 1944.

house. As Mark Girouard has written, The Red House, 'provided the "Queen Anne" answer to the problem of designing a London terrace house. The Red House was to be very widely imitated, inside and out, but this was not because it was strikingly original, but because it could be imitated easily'.[122]

Contemporaries certainly admired it; Mary Eliza Haweis wrote in her artful little book on *Beautiful Houses* that, 'The "*Red House*", with its handsome russet façade and niche holding a *Nankeen* vase, has been so continually parodied by cheap builders possessed by the idea that red brick, a blue pot, and a fat sunflower in the window are all that is necessary to be fashionably aesthetic and *Queen Anne*, that it is a mercy the original house still stands to point a wholesome moral'.[123]

Unfortunately the Red House no longer stands; badly damaged by a flying bomb in 1944, it was demolished in the early 1950s.

NO. 180, QUEEN'S GATE, SOUTH KENSINGTON was a notably fine 'Queen Anne' house, built in 1884–85 for Henry Francis Makins. It was designed by that pioneer and master of the style, Richard Norman Shaw, who adapted the usual façade treatment to a corner site, artfully placing the porch to straddle the corner and making the side elevation dramatic with two tall chimney stacks. Inside, the house was originally decorated and furnished by Morris & Co.

The fate of this house was one of the Victorian Society's earliest cases as it was threatened by the

▼ No.180 Queen's Gate, South Kensington.

▶ The Tower House in Bedford Park, photographed by Bedford Lemere from further west in Bedford Road in the 1880s; the houses in the foreground survive.

expansion of Imperial College, which had already done away with the Imperial Institute (see page 127). As reported in 1970, 'The Society appealed to the architects for the rebuilding, Messrs Norman and Dawbarn, as long ago as 1958 when they were told that it was too late to do anything about the plans!' Yet the house proudly stood for another decade when, with more historic building legislation and the need to reapply for planning permission, there seemed to be some hope for it.

Despite pressure from the Victorian Society and a press campaign, Imperial College destroyed the house in 1970. 'An attempt by the Secretary to persuade the Registrar to save at least some of the magnificent fireplaces came to nothing; everything that was saved had to be bought from the demolishers during the demolition. Many fine things have been lost'.[124] Such is the typical behaviour of institutions of education. At least the Society had more success a few years later in saving Norman Shaw's earlier house at no. 196, Queen's Gate, from the expansion plans of the Royal College of Art.

Norman Shaw was the architect who created the 'Queen Anne' character of Bedford Park, the 'first garden suburb' created by Jonathan T. Carr to the west of Hammersmith. Shaw designed the church,

the shops and many of the fashionable 'Queen Anne' houses, including the one built for himself by the slightly dodgy developer. THE TOWER HOUSE in Bedford Road was designed in 1878. With its 16 rooms, it was much larger and more prominent than any of the other houses; it had two generous projecting bays facing the extensive gardens, a cupola – the 'tower' – surmounting its pitched roof and very tall brick chimneys.

'In the house,' wrote T. Affleck Greeves, 'Carr had a small business room where, as "Lord of the Manor", he used to deal with the affairs of Bedford Park, with which he remained closely concerned. An energetic and genial man, he seemed to be perpetually short of money, and to lose friends as quickly as he made them; his house was the scene of lavish entertainments, which he could ill afford'.[125]

After 1908, the Tower House was a convent school. It was demolished in about 1931 and replaced by St Catherine's Court, a block of flats of no architectural merit or character. It was unfortunate that this fine house went so long before the rehabilitation of Bedford Park following the listing of most of the surviving houses in 1967, for the suburb is now lacking a much-needed second architectural focus.

▲ The dining room and the garden elevation of 'Rance's Folly' in Cambridge in c.1880.

Thomas Jeckyll was one of the most intriguing of Victorian architects. He designed spiky Gothic churches, was an early enthusiast for the art of Japan, was an inspired designer of ironwork, furniture and interiors, and is today perhaps best known for the Peacock Room over-painted by Whistler, now in Washington DC.

Jeckyll's largest domestic commission was for a house in the middle of a terrace in ST ANDREW'S STREET, near the centre of CAMBRIDGE. Built in 1870–72, it was designed for a solicitor and future Mayor of Cambridge, Henry Rance, and, because of its distinct oddness, soon became known as 'Rance's Folly'. The tall, five-storey house towered over its modest neighbours. The exterior was an austere and awkward interpretation of the new 'Queen Anne' manner, with dressings in bright red brick. Both elevations were oddly asymmetrical and there was a two-storey, curved projecting bay facing the gardens.

The interior was grand and technologically advanced. There was a lift, as many as four bathrooms and a swimming pool. Jeckyll designed the interiors in his idiosyncratic Aesthetic manner and the dining room had a remarkable 'Mathematical Ceiling' treated with arcs of circles and ornamented in the new Japanese taste. No. 62 St Andrew's Street was later acquired by Cambridge University's Board of Estate Management and, despite some local protest, was demolished in 1957.

An architect-designed house for a successful artist which incorporated a studio became a distinct new building type by the 1870s. Norman Shaw designed several, both in Hampstead and in Melbury Road, Kensington. But the more avant-garde artists preferred Tite Street in Chelsea, running north from the new Chelsea Embankment. And here Edward William Godwin designed several studio-houses, whose advanced design upset the authorities.

The celebrated WHITE HOUSE was designed for the painter James McNeill Whistler. Godwin had by now adopted a mannered and austere version of the 'Queen Anne' style. His first design, made in 1877, envisaged a low, two-storey street elevation, of white brick and Portland stone, above which rose a large mansard roof of green tiles enclosing the rear-facing studio. This was far too austere for the Metropolitan Board of Works, which declined to grant a lease unless more

The White House in Tite Street, Chelsea, photographed by Sydney Newbery in the 1950s.

ornament was applied to the façade – thus subsequently fuelling the myth of Godwin as a proto-modernist, ahead of his time.

The interior was designed by Godwin in the Japanese taste with carefully chosen colours. In the event, however, Whistler had little time to enjoy his house before he was obliged to sell it in 1879, having been made bankrupt by his libel action against Ruskin. The White House was then bought by the art critic Harry Quilter, who spoiled it. Nevertheless, Godwin's very special house

survived largely intact until 1963 when it was demolished by its owner, the Hon. Colin Tennant, the wealthy socialite friend of Princess Margaret. This act of gratuitous vandalism was permitted despite the association with Whistler and the fact that the house was listed at Grade II. Only the Chelsea Society seems to have protested, arguing, 'It is clear that the White House has an overwhelming claim to be considered as a building of historic interest' and that, 'Although architectural feeling in the present day would find

Tite Street looking north, with Chelsea Lodge on the left and the White House on the right; from a postcard of c.1900.

much sympathy with Godwin's original design, it must not be assumed that the house as altered was in any way undesirable as a residence. It had great charm and was very comfortable. It owes its destruction to the fact that it stands on a double plot of land and is therefore "developable".[126]

Tennant, subsequently Baron Glenconner, built a Neo-Georgian house for himself on the northern half of the site.

Godwin designed other interesting studio houses nearby. CHELSEA LODGE, NO. 60 TITE STREET was a double studio house on the opposite side of the street, designed in 1878 for Archibald Stuart Wortley and the cartoonist Carlo Pellegrini. This was more conventionally 'Queen Anne' and the Metropolitan Board of Works was mollified. As *Building News* reported the following year, this house 'had nothing in common with Mr Whistler's house. It is a plain Old English type of house, with mullioned casements and 17th century detail'.[127] This corner house was later altered by the artist Edwin Abbey and replaced after 1937 by a Neo-Georgian block of flats.

The Arts and Crafts architect, designer, conservationist and socialist idealist, Charles Robert Ashbee, designed several unusual houses along Cheyne Walk in Chelsea. The earliest was NO. 37 CHEYNE WALK, known as the MAGPIE & STUMP, the name of a notorious pub, which had stood on the site until it was burnt out in 1886.

Ashbee's Magpie & Stump was his first building, erected in 1893–94 for himself, his mother – now estranged from his merchant and pornographer father – and his sisters. The exterior was of brick, with a triple-height projecting oriel bay of unusual shape modelled on that of the timber front of Sir Paul Pindar's house in Bishopsgate, recently taken down (and now in the Victoria & Albert Museum). Inside, the house was complicated and imaginative, enriched with furniture and decoration designed by Ashbee, electric light fittings by W.A.S. Benson and much more, making extensive use of enamel and embossed leather; in the opinion of his biographer, Alan Crawford, it was the most interesting of Ashbee's interiors.

A few years later the Magpie & Stump was joined by two more houses by Ashbee: nos. 38 and

▲ C.R. Ashbee's house, the 'Magpie & Stump' in Chelsea, with No.38 Cheyne Walk, its surviving neighbour by Ashbee, on the left; photograph by Röder of Leipzig from *Neubauten in London* published by Wasmuth in Berlin in 1900.

39 Cheyne Walk. Today, they are the only survivors of Ashbee's contributions to Chelsea. The interior of No. 37 had survived intact until the death of the last owner in 1964; the Victorian society then intervened to prevent his executors from stripping it out and since discovered that the whole house was threatened by a proposal by Wates Ltd to build a six-storey block of flats on the corner of Oakley Street. This was opposed by the Greater London Council as well as by the Victorian Society, but at the public inquiry held in 1965 it was suggested that, after a meeting with Norman Wates, the society's chairman, Nikolaus Pevsner, had suggested that No. 37 was not as good a building as No. 38 or No. 39. Horrified by this misinterpretation, Pevsner insisted, 'The style to which No. 37 belongs is one which the continent and the United States avidly adopted. Good buildings representing it are getting

terribly rare. This is why I would greatly regret [its] disappearance.' But then he added, foolishly and fatally, 'If No. 37 were to be replaced by something architecturally better, I might give in.'

In the event, Ashbee's house was demolished in 1968, along with its older neighbours to the east, after 'a thoroughly specious decision by the Secretary of State. In its place now stands the end of a block of luxury flats, wholly out of scale with the buildings in Cheyne Walk'.[128] As the development site was large, it is clear that the retention of the Magpie & Stump would not have greatly impeded matters.

Ashbee's other built contribution to Chelsea faced the Thames further west. NOS. 71–75 CHEYNE WALK was a varied and picturesque group of brick houses built by the architect between 1897 and 1912. With their different rooflines and seemingly arbitrary pattern of fenestration, they were full of subtle allusions to both Old Chelsea and Old London – with which Ashbee, as a founder of what became the Survey of London, was much concerned. They lasted until April 1941, when they were destroyed by the same land mine that obliterated Chelsea Old Church.

Ashbee's biographer, Alan Crawford, records how the architect Sydney Castle visited the site and 'found himself in front of a mass of rubble between Old Church Street and Danvers Street: "Those

fronts," he wrote, "those oddly fascinating fronts which aped nothing Chelsea and yet seemed to breathe its atmosphere so intensely – gone!"'[129]

After the war, the church was reconstructed but a public garden replaced Ashbee's houses.

In GLASGOW, Alexander 'Greek' Thomson had treated the problem of the urban terrace in a very different manner. The tenement was a traditional building type in Scotland and the basic building block for the 19th-century city. As far as Francis Worsdall, the historian of the Glasgow tenement, was concerned, 'The only really original contribution to tenement design was that of Alexander Thomson, who revolutionised the standard elevation by linking its isolated elements in a manner at once masterly, and entirely his own'.[130]

In the 1960s and later most of Thomson's tenements were unfortunately demolished by the authorities, along with so many others capable of rehabilitation, in misguided attempts at slum clearance. These included his finest and most influential, QUEEN'S PARK TERRACE, which went as late as 1980–81 despite being listed Category 'A'. Begun in 1856, its very long façade was repetitive yet a distinctive subtle rhythm was established by recessions in the wall plane and by the alternation between window lintels and connecting string course on the second floor. The northern end was distinguished by a corner window tower with concave facets reminiscent of a fluted column – a feature possibly inspired by the Temple of Venus at Baalbek.

After the usual neglect, this extraordinary building was compulsorily purchased and destroyed by Glasgow Council. 'The work of demolition began on St Andrew's Day 1980,' noted Worsdall. 'To demolish one of the treasures of Scottish architecture by Scotland's greatest architect, on Scotland's national day, seems to me to be deliberately perverse. It is, however, typical of the attitude of the District Council, which frequently shows a disregard of the wishes of those who know and love this sadly dismembered city'.[131] The site remains empty.

Two other examples of Thomson's brilliance at façade design abutted and enhanced his first ecclesiastical masterpiece, the Caledonia Road Church south of the Clyde (see page 18). Each was a masterly exercise in ordering fenestration while playing with wall planes and balancing the verticals of square piers against the horizontals created by the use of 'pseudo-isodomic' masonry. Both were built, along with the church, in 1856–57. NOS. 190–192 HOSPITAL STREET was demolished in 1972 and NOS. 37–39 CATHCART ROAD cleared the following year. The sites remain empty, and thanks to malevolent neglect by Glasgow Corporation, the Caledonia Road Church gutted by arsonists in 1965.

One of the most influential examples of urban domestic design was the BISHOP'S HOUSE in

▲ The remarkable southern corner of Queen's Park Terrace, Eglinton Street, Glasgow, photographed by Colin McWilliam in 1980.

◀ Pugin's Bishop's House in Birmingham, on the corner of Weaman Street and Bath Street, in 1958.

▼ The Bishop's House in Birmingham, seen from the south in Shadwell Street in 1959 with Pugin's St Chad's Cathedral on the left.

▲▶ The garden front and the entrance hall of Druid's Cross House in Liverpool, photographed in 1971.

Bath Street, BIRMINGHAM, which A.W.N. Pugin built for Bishop Walsh in 1840–41, diagonally opposite St Chad's Roman Catholic Cathedral. It was a brilliant, experimental essay in creating a modern Gothic urban vernacular, at once picturesque and rational. Built entirely of red brick, it had two asymmetrical gabled wings framing a small courtyard, which came forward right to the boundaries of the site. Massive chimneybreasts grew out of the walls and the varied fenestration reflected the position and functions of the spaces within.

This rational simplification of Gothic forms was to be continued by Butterfield, Street, Scott and so many other Victorian architects. An attempt to save this remarkable building was made by the newly founded Victorian Society, but the decision to demolish had already been taken. The Bishop's House was cleared in 1960 to build Birmingham's disastrous Inner Ring Road, which now sweeps past the entrance to Pugin's St Chad's Cathedral. As his Rosemary Hill remarks, this was 'one of the worst losses, not only among Pugin's work but to Victorian architecture'.[132]

Harvey Lonsdale Elmes, the brilliant young architect of St George's Hall in LIVERPOOL, sometimes employed Gothic as an alternative to his Graeco-Roman monumental Classic, but for one of his few villas he designed in the Italianate manner. DRUIDS CROSS HOUSE in Woolton, outside Liverpool was designed for Joseph Hornby, a Liverpool merchant and alderman, and completed in 1847 – the year of his architect's premature death. It took its name from the Calder Stones, the Neolithic megaliths now in nearby Calderstone Park.

Like so many villas in their grounds in the city's suburbs, Druids Cross was threatened in the 1960s by the proposed development of its grounds. In 1972, an application for listed building consent for demolition was opposed by the Victorian Society and supported by the Georgian Group and the Merseyside Civic Society. Before the case could go to public inquiry, the application was withdrawn and proposals made for converting the house into flats. The proposed changes to this now-neglected and decaying building were not considered satisfactory, however nothing was done. A few years later, a new application for demolition was made. Listed building consent was then granted subject to certain architectural details being salvaged, but as the society reported in 1978, 'Regrettably the developer (Winward) and the demolition contractor (Leabreck) failed to comply with the conditions, and the interior details were

smashed during demolition. Both were found guilty and fined in the Magistrates Court'. The site is now covered with modern houses.

CLEVELEY in ALLERTON – another leafy suburb of LIVERPOOL – was designed by George Gilbert Scott in his secular Gothic manner owing much to the example of Pugin. The stone mansion was built in Allerton Road, in 1865 for Joseph Leather, a cotton merchant, in an area full of substantial merchants' houses. Scott broke up the principal elevation with a series of gabled bays projected to different extents. The generous

windows, divided by tall, round shafts with carved capitals, exemplified Scott's belief that modern improvements, like plate glass, could easily be incorporated into the Gothic style.

Along with other houses, Cleveley was demolished in 1965, thus making the Allerton Road area, as Pevsner discovered, 'a document of senseless destruction'.[133] Cleveley Road lined with modern suburban houses now covers the site; Scott's lodge and stables, however, survive.

Edward Buckton Lamb was one of Goodhart-Rendel's 'Rogue Architects'. His ecclesiastical

◁ St Martin's Vicarage in Allcroft Road, Gospel Oak, photographed in 1969 shortly before demolition.

▲ St Clement's Vicarage in Boscombe, Bournemouth, photographed by Herbert Felton in 1943, with the church alongside.

masterpiece, centrally planned and covered by a wildly inventive timber roof, was St Martin's Church in Gospel Oak, north London. ST MARTIN'S VICARAGE was built at the same time, in 1864–66, close by in Allcroft Road, which was named after the donor of the church. Like the church, the vicarage was built of Kentish rag stone and displayed the idiosyncrasy of the architect in the way the central bay projected above the ground-floor tripartite window and in the general oddness of the design.

A century later, the vicarage, along with the neighbouring school (not by Lamb) and St Martin's Church itself all found themselves in the middle of a comprehensive redevelopment area. As the Victorian Society reported in 1970, 'The church remains; the Vicarage could have, too, but neither Camden Council, nor the GLC nor the Ministry were prepared to insist that it should be conserved as a notable feature (with the church) in an otherwise redeveloped area'.[134] As the section of street where the vicarage stood remains unaltered (albeit gratuitously renamed), it is clear

that the loss of this odd, but most endearing house could easily have been avoided.

ST CLEMENT'S Church and VICARAGE at BOSCOMBE, Bournemouth, Hampshire were designed by John Dando Sedding (who married the first vicar's sister). Although quite different in style, both buildings were progressive designs at the time. The church, built in 1871–73 (with a later tower by Sedding and his successor, Henry Wilson), was in the English Late Gothic manner being pursued by Bodley and G.G. Scott junior; the Vicarage, built in 1873–74, in the new domestic 'Queen Anne' vernacular style of Richard Norman Shaw. The Vicarage was connected to the church by a covered way.

Along with the nearby school and cottages by Sedding and the Convent of the Sisters of Bethany, designed by Shaw himself, these buildings 'formed a unique group, a late-Victorian pioneering design' in the opinion of the Victorian Society. The Society was then lobbying on behalf of the long-neglected church, which survives today. But the charming vicarage, together with the Oratory attached to the church, were demolished in 1965 to be replaced by the sort of ordinary modern suburban house preferred by the Church Commissioners for the clergy. It is not even properly linked to Sedding's covered way. 'If such a building can slip unobserved through planning controls,' the Society observed, 'anything can'.[135]

Huge numbers of suburban villas were built in the 19th century. Comparatively few were designed by named architects, but the story of their evolution from the Greek and Italianate villas of the Regency to the substantial detached picturesque Gothic mid-Victorian houses, which created the character of so many new, middle-class suburbs, is a fascinating one. Many have gone, often because more houses could be built on their comparatively large sites in the 20th century, but also because of the prejudice against such buildings, fuelled by a belief that they were gloomy, inconvenient and expensive to heat. Only a few, rather more special examples can be illustrated here.

'HIAWATHA' in Goldington Road, BEDFORD was built for himself by local architect John Usher – apparently the first Victorian in the town

to grow a beard, who 'seems to have made quite a study of the beard as the natural adornment and protection of man'.[136] The house, named after the popular poem, *The Song of Hiawatha*, by the American poet Longfellow and published in 1855, was both typical and extreme. Like so many other contemporary villas, it was asymmetrical composed around a tower and had prominent gables with ornamental timber bargeboards.

Usher, however, was clearly influenced by contemporary experiments in Ruskinian or Continentally-inspired Gothic; the brickwork was polychromatic and certain features, like the stubby corner column on the tower and the triangular trefoil windows, suggest admiration for the eccentric motifs used by 'Rogue' architects such as Bassett Keeling. Similar motifs could be found in the design for houses designed by George Truefitt in north London which, as it happened, were being published as *Villa & Cottage Architecture* by Blackie & Son between 1865 and 1868.

Hiawatha was demolished a century later, in 1968, by a consortium of developers who had bought it to redevelop the site with a banal office block called Zurich House.

'WESTHOLME' in Overton Road, CHELTENHAM, was another High Victorian Gothic villa designed by an architect for himself. It was the creation of John Middleton, who was born in York, moved to Cheltenham and clearly had no sympathy with the general Classical character of the Regency spa town. 'Westholme' was designed in 1866 and was full of the qualities described by High Victorian Gothicists as Vigour and 'Go!'. The house sported such mannerisms as corbelled-out chimneybreasts, laterally flush buttresses and a strange oriel over the arched entrance, which came to a point. Like Usher's villa in Bedford, its composition was based around a squat tower which sorted strange windows – this time small and round – but it was built of monochrome rubble-stone rather than multi-coloured brickwork. Inside, as Middleton's biographer records,

the house resembled something from an Arthurian legend with beautifully carved stone and plasterwork; Gothic ornamentation; carvings in stone of angels just above eye level; Morris and Burne-Jones tiles surrounded the fireplaces; ceiling panels in Oregon pine, rich and brown-red, with paper transfer work in green, cream and gold. The whole effect was Mediaeval, romantic and sumptuous with some intriguing innovations designed by Middleton himself.

▲ 'Westholme' in Overton Road, Cheltenham, photographed by Nigel Temple in 1973 (perspective corrected).

Later renamed 'Abbeyholme', this rather special house became a rest home soon after the Second World War (when a photograph of it was used as representative of '1860' in Lionel Brett's Penguin book on *The Things We See: Houses*). In 1973, it was demolished in favour of a block of flats. This was not without protest, but by the time the Victorian Society learned of the threat, permission had already been granted by the local authority and the building was not listed despite being described in the *Buildings of England* volume. Some of the fine interior fittings were salvaged by Cheltenham Art Gallery and Museum, and by the Bowes Museum in County Durham.

'ALLENBANK' in CAMDEN ROAD, London, was a villa designed in 1863 by the obscure architect Henry Hodge. It was conventional in its asymmetrical com-position, but unusual – in London – being in a sort of Scottish Baronial style, with a tall round turret or tourelle rising above the entrance, as well as a crow-stepped gable. For some reason, an early photograph of this house attracted the attention of several authors wanting to illustrate a typically elaborate mid-Victorian villa, perhaps because it might seem to resemble a miniature Balmoral Castle.[137] This did not prevent the house's destruction in the 1960s.

One of the best areas for an enjoyable variety of mid-Victorian villas was SYDENHAM in south London, where development was encouraged by the advent of the re-erected Crystal Palace, as well as by the new railways. Many were designed by the firm of Banks & Barry, Charles Barry junior being surveyor to the large Dulwich Estate and architect of the new Dulwich College buildings erected in 1866–70. Contemporary with those was one of the best and most prominent of the villas.

THE KNOLL was erected in about 1870, near the summit of Sydenham Hill, close to Paxton's vast iron-and-glass creation and right above the tunnel portico from which emerged the railway running in a brick-arched lined cutting into Crystal Palace

High Level Station. The tall, red-brick villa was designed in a vaguely Gothic style, its four-storey bay flanked by a conservatory overlooking the railway lines. The Crystal Palace burned down in 1936 (see page 32); the railway closed in 1954 and the splendid station, designed by Barry's

▶ Part of the entrance front of 'Lululaund' designed by H.H. Richardson, with the gates added by Giles Gilbert Scott, photographed in c.1906.

brother, came down in 1961 (see page 52), leaving the neglected and forlorn villa as a last, still impressive relic of the optimistic Victorian magnificence once here. In the course of the process by which so many such fine and solid villas were replaced by unimpressive new housing developments and blocks of flats, almost exactly a century after it was built, The Knoll disappeared.

One of the saddest losses of Victorian domestic architecture was that of LULULAUND, the home of the Sir Hubert von Herkomer in the village of BUSHEY, Hertfordshire. The house was named after Lulu Griffiths, second wife of the Anglo-German painter; it was grander than a suburban

'Lululaund' at Bushey soon after completion of the house; from a postcard.

villa and more remarkable than the studio-houses designed by Norman Shaw, E.W. Godwin and others for successful painters. Above all, it was unique as the only work in Britain by the great American architect Henry Hobson Richardson, whose architecture owed much to, but brilliantly transcended British High-Victorian Gothic.

Born in Bavaria, but trained in South Kensington as well as in Munich, Herkomer achieved fame both for his social realist canvases and for his portraits. He encountered Richardson in the United States when he painted his portrait in 1886. The architect died later that year, but not before he provided the painter with a design for the façade of his proposed house in lieu of a fee. As built of white Bavarian tufa and red sandstone, this powerful elevation had all the rich texture, colour contrasts and solid massiveness of Richardson's American buildings. Like them, it was designed in Richardson's own version of French Romanesque but with unusual features such as the wide segmental arch, which straddled and wrapped around two round, turreted towers.

It was Herkomer, however, who had made the plan of the house and it was he who was responsible for the rather Germanic treatment of the interiors completed in 1894. They must have

◄ The drawing room at 'Lululaund'; from *Hubert von Herkomer, R.A.: A Study and a Biography* by A.L. Baldry published in 1901.

been amazing. The hall and staircase were lined with huge panels of redwood; his bedroom had a copper ceiling and walls covered in gold leaf; the dining room was decorated with a relief frieze of female figures painted by the artist and the great drawing room had a music gallery and a vast arched chimneypiece with interlaced mouldings.

Despite the somewhat lugubrious character of his paintings, Herkomer was an enthusiast for the new. He was keen on electric light and motor cars, and planned Lululaund so as to make the house practical. Herkomer did much for Bushey, establishing an art school in the village; he also built a theatre in the grounds of the house, where he staged influential 'pictorial-music-plays'; later this was used as a cinema as Herkomer directed and acted in some of the earliest commercial films to be made in Britain.

Honoured by both King Edward VII and Kaiser Wilhelm II, Herkomer's remarkable career exemplified the close cultural ties that existed between Britain and Germany in the 19th century.

Perhaps it was a mercy that he died in 1914, just before the outbreak of the world war that would release the hatreds that poisoned so much of the rest of the century. After that war, Lululaund was used for a time by the Bushey Film Corporation before being allowed to fall into dereliction. A local businessman bought the house and offered to give it to Bushey District Council for use as a museum, but anti-German feeling militated against saving it and the house was pulled down in 1939 on the eve of another world war and its grounds eventually developed. Mercifully, a small portion of Richardson's façade was allowed to survive – the massive, elaborate front door and its tympanum – which is now the entrance to a club isolated among the suburban houses of Melbourne Road and which still testifies to the genius of one of the greatest of American architects. As Sir Nikolaus Pevsner, another German who did even more for his adopted country, wrote soon after the war about this poignant fragment, 'It must at all costs be preserved'.[138]

10: COUNTRY HOUSES

Country houses were among the most elaborate and expensive examples of Victorian architecture. They were the buildings which were regarded most seriously by contemporaries in terms of both status and design, and they became the expressions of Victorian attitudes and taste which the 20th century found most hideous and ridiculous – as the quotation from P.G. Wodehouse with which this book began suggests. A surprising number of country houses were built or rebuilt in the Victorian period by both the old landed aristocracy and by new money anxious to establish a more elevated position in society. This process reached a peak in the 1870s, after which the long agricultural depression began to militate against country-house building. Although their origins, in terms of planning, use and style, can be traced further back, the tradition of country-house building reached its apotheosis in the reign of Victoria (who, of course, with her husband, built her own, both in the Isle of Wight and in Scotland).

Victorian country houses were bigger, more solidly built, more elaborate and complex, and, on the whole, more lavishly furnished and decorated than those built in earlier centuries. They were planned for an ordered way of life, with immense care taken to ensure that different classes and sexes did not come into contact and that kitchen smells would not reach the dining room. Technical improvements in plumbing, lighting and servicing made them more comfortable – and by contemporary standards, more efficient than in the past. As Mark Girouard wrote in *The Victorian Country House*, his classic study of the building type back in 1971,

> Seldom can so much money and such exhaustive study have produced a group of buildings that, as private houses, became so soon and painfully obsolete. Remarkably few big Victorian country houses are still privately lived in; and it is largely thanks to the English system of private education that so many remain in existence at all.[139]

Clouds in Wiltshire, renowned as a political power-house and social centre, so carefully and expensively designed by Philip Webb to unite tradition and modernity, was lived in for little

◀◀ The ground floor corridor at Eaton Hall, photographed by G.B. Mason in 1959.

over 40 years before it was sold, cut down in size and mutilated to make it suitable for institutional use. Alfred Waterhouse's Eaton Hall, which cost the Duke of Westminster well over half a million pounds – a colossal sum – has gone altogether.

To modern eyes, it is usually the smaller houses which seem more architecturally significant and it was with these, whether urban, suburban or rural, that the better-known Victorian architects were involved. Many large Victorian country houses may seem rambling, confused and mediocre, and were often designed by rather dim architects. But there were architects of distinction, like Anthony Salvin and William Burn and, later, Webb, Norman Shaw and Ernest George, who specialised in country-house design. Earlier examples were designed in the Italian Classical manner or in the picturesque styles that had suitable historical and romantic associations: Elizabethan, Jacobean and Mediaeval.

Most of the serious, assertively masculine High Victorian houses were, of course, Gothic. Then later in the century the more eclectic and less ponderous 'Old English' and 'Queen Anne' styles became fashionable. By the end of the century, the Arts and Crafts influence was inspiring beautifully crafted houses, which cleverly combined local building traditions with modern planning, but by then the country house was becoming less the social centre of local life and the centre of an agricultural estate as a house to commute to for weekend entertaining.

The Great War, with the slaughter of so many sons and heirs, began to undermine the stability of so many country houses. Victorian houses, in particular, began to seem too large, unsuited to changed social and economic conditions and, as taste changed, simply hideous. As a more recent historian of the building type, Michael Hall, has observed,

> Conceived by so many of their patrons as the backdrop to happy family life and rural improvement, for most of the twentieth century such buildings were regarded as the gloomy architectural relics of a feudal caste that had no place in modern life.[140]

Victorian country houses were probably too specialised; certainly they were difficult to run with fewer servants. 'Perhaps the most "obsolete" of all English buildings,' wrote John Summerson in 1942, considering the future of wartime Britain's architectural heritage, 'are the great country houses whose owners can no longer afford to live in them'.[141]

Along with so many country houses of earlier centuries, many never recovered from being requisitioned in the Second World War and were never lived in again. Many more were demolished in the great post-war holocaust of country houses that reached a terrible crescendo in the early 1950s. And many Victorian houses that survived were shorn of their outbuildings and mutilated internally.

Given the prejudice against their architecture combined with the collapse of the economic and social system that sustained them, it is perhaps surprising that any Victorian country houses still stand at all. In fact, a large number of good examples do survive, albeit usually in institutional use. Although Wightwick Manor in Staffordshire fortuitously fell into the hands of the National Trust as long ago as 1937, it was not until the 1970s that serious efforts were made to protect and restore outstanding examples of Victorian country houses as buildings worthy of preservation and study.

Soon after the publication of his book, Girouard was asked by the National Trust to make a list of Victorian houses in England, which, with their intact furnishings and collections, it should seek to acquire if ever they came on to the market. His six top 'musts' were Cragside, Tyntesfield, Brodsworth Hall, Thoresby Hall, Mentmore Towers and Alnwick Castle. Today all still stand; two are owned by the Trust, one by English Heritage, two are hotels and one is still lived in. Even so, there is a much longer list of houses of real distinction which have gone – and, unlike the case with other types of Victorian architecture – none as a result of enemy action.

TRENTHAM HALL in Staffordshire disappeared remarkably early, that is, even before the Great War, although it had for a time been the principal English seat of the immensely wealthy Duke of Sutherland. Designed by Sir Charles Barry in his best Italianate

◁ Trentham Hall in Staffordshire from the gardens in c.1906.

manner and built in 1834–49, with terraces and a formal garden overlooking a lake, it was one of several large country houses on large estates (five in Scotland) owned by the 2nd Duke. Trentham was abandoned in 1906, partly because industrial pollution in the area south of Stoke-on-Trent was making the lake unpleasant. As no institutional use could be found for it, and agreement could not be reached with either the County Council or the Borough of Stoke-on-Trent to take it on, a sale of the contents was held in 1907 and almost all of the house demolished four years later.

Although he retained the grounds and opened them to the public, the 4th Duke would not tolerate interference over the disposal of his property. As became clear after the war with the 'private palaces' in London, the great aristocratic families were quite happy to demolish fine and historic buildings if it was in their financial interest to do so: noblesse would certainly not oblige over architecture, whatever the State or public might think.

MOUNT FELIX at Walton-on-Thames in Surrey was rather smaller than Trentham, but was also by Barry, who enlarged a Georgian house for the Earl of Tankerville in 1837–40 and gave it a

▼ Mount Felix at Walton-on-Thames in Surrey with the campanile added by Charles Barry, photographed by Herbert Felton in 1958.

fine campanile-cum-porte-cochère. This Italianate house, already divided into flats, was described as 'threatened with demolition' in the Victorian Society's first annual report after it had been bought by a speculator. Wholly predictably, it was badly damaged by fire in 1965 after its condition was allowed to deteriorate.

The following year the Society reported that, 'In the circumstances the Society has not been able to question Surrey County Council's approval of demolition – but a building of such importance ought never to have been allowed to reach such a state'.[142]

BAYONS MANOR in Lincolnshire was a romantic mediaeval fantasy already doomed when the Victorian Society was founded. It was built by Charles Tennyson d'Eyncourt, uncle of the poet Alfred Tennyson, who added a suffix to his surname to hint at the desired antiquity of his lineage. He inherited a Regency house in 1835 and immediately set about converting into a romantic castle with the help of the architect William Adams Nicholson. Battlements, a tower and a wing with a great hall were added; later, a moat, outer walls and a gatehouse with a drawbridge completed the vision, together with a ruined keep, built on a mound in 1842. The interior was an antiquarian assemblage of armour, heraldry and stained glass.

As Mark Girouard explained, 'The literary equivalents of Bayons are the novels of Walter Scott and still more of Charles d'Eyncourt's friend, Bulwer Lytton, who wrote *Harold: The Last of the Saxon Kings* (1848) during a stay there.' Tennyson d'Eyncourt's descendants sold the house after the Second World War and it was never lived in again. The new owner bought it only for the land and the house fell victim to vandalism and neglect. It was finally blown up in 1965.

The decay and destruction of the house was a sad end to his dynastic ambitions; but at least it meant that for a few years Bayons became far more picturesque than he could ever have dreamed of, indeed more beautiful and more romantic than many a genuine ruined castle.[143]

The verdant landscape around the Wiltshire village of Fonthill Gifford is full of the ghosts of lost houses. There were six country houses in the area bearing the name Fonthill – variously Fonthill House, Fonthill Splendens and Fonthill Abbey – all of them now demolished. Three dated from the 19th century. The most celebrated, of

◀ The south front of the second, Victorian, Fonthill Abbey, photographed in c.1901 for *Country Life*.

course, was James Wyatt's Fonthill Abbey, the early Gothic Revival prodigy built by William Beckford, almost entirely demolished after the central tower collapsed in 1825.

Twenty years later part of Beckford's former estate was bought by Richard Grosvenor, Marquess of Westminster, who proposed to build a new FONTHILL ABBEY, near the site of the old one. His architect was the Edinburgh-born William Burn, the doyen of country-house architects of his generation. Burn had been in the vanguard in the revival of the Jacobean style – both English and Scottish – but his greatest talent was as a planner. As David Walker has written,

> He played a central role in the transition of the country house from the rigid formality of the eighteenth century to the comfortable asymmetry of the nineteenth. Above all, he was adept at reconciling the conflicting requirements of his clients – for grandeur, privacy, outlook, guests' accommodation, logistic convenience and segregation of servicing. Indeed, his thinking on how buildings should function was on a more sophisticated level than that of any previous British architect.[144]

For the great palace he first designed for his immensely wealthy aristocratic client, Burn proposed to import a new Franco-Scottish style he had developed: that turreted, castle-like Early Renaissance style, which came to be known as 'Scottish Baronial'. In the event, the house that was built in 1856–59 was rather smaller, but still a pioneering example of Scottish Baronial in England, with crow-stepped gables flanked by tourelles, but given a modern touch with projecting ground-floor bays equipped with sash windows, using large sheets of plate glass.

Fonthill Abbey passed by descent to the Shaw-Stewart family. It was requisitioned by the Army in 1940 and roughly treated; by the early 1950s it was in poor repair. The house was demolished in 1955 by its new owner, John Granville Morrison, whose family had by now acquired most of the Fonthill Estate. It would not be the last Victorian country house at Fonthill that this serial vandal would destroy (see also page 185). The stables and terraces survive, however, and a new house has more recently been created here, incorporating the ballroom added to Deene Park in Northamptonshire by Lord Cardigan of Charge of the Light Brigade notoriety.

▶ Craigends, Renfrewshire, in ruins in 1966.

William Burn's chief clerk and subsequent partner in his Edinburgh office was David Bryce, who developed an- independent country-house practice and became a master at Scottish Baronial. It was a style derived from 16th- and 17th-century Scottish castles, but one with a distinct modern character of its own. And it was a style which the 20th century has not looked upon kindly. Many found it ridiculous: Osbert Lancaster could write in 1938 that it was,

as the name implies, essentially an upper-class style and one which mirrored faithfully that passion on the part of the nobility and gentry for combining the minimum of comfort with the maximum of expense that has always exercised so great an influence over our domestic architecture. Spiral staircases of a steepness and gloom that rendered oubliettes unnecessary; small windows which made up for the amount of light they kept out·by the amount of wind they let in; drains which conformed to mediaeval standards with an accuracy which in the rest of the structure remained an eagerly desired, but as yet unattained ideal.[145]

This was neither true nor fair, but in Scotland prejudice against the style combined with an enthusiasm for wiping out tangible remains of the Victorian past (often with dynamite) led to the disappearance of many of Bryce's finest creations. As the organisers of an exhibition held in 1976 to mark the centenary of Bryce's death concluded:

At his best Bryce was a designer of both power and quality, a man whose known works already exceed 200 and to whom the major commissions of Victorian Scotland came one by one almost as of a right. A hundred years later he is an architect pursued almost relentlessly by destruction and by demolition.[146]

CRAIGENDS, near Johnstone in Renfrewshire, was one of the very best examples of Scottish Baronial. It was built in 1857 for Alexander Cunninghame. The principal feature of the asymmetrical stone exterior was a tall, projecting bay modelled on the central tower of Fyvie Castle, with a recess under an arch between the tourelles flanking the gable; other elements were derived from Maybole Castle. There was a large conservatory and the interior had Jacobean ceilings and an Elizabethan panelled oak library.

By 1966, Craigends was ruinous. As the house is not far from Glasgow, a new institutional use for it was surely possible but it was demolished

instead the following year. A private housing estate now occupies the site.

EATON HALL in Cheshire was one of the most expensive country houses ever built in real terms. It cost £600,000, but the owner – Hugh Lupus Grosvenor, Marquess of Westminster, who was elevated to a dukedom in 1874 – could well afford it from the income from his landholdings in Mayfair, London and elsewhere. When he inherited in 1869, his Cheshire seat was an unfashionable exercise in Regency Gothic by William Porden, which had been altered by William Burn. The new Marquess felt obliged to rebuild and chose as his architect not a specialist in country houses, but the rising star of the earnest High-Victorian Gothic Revival, Alfred Waterhouse, who had recently won the competition for Manchester Town Hall.

Waterhouse was a brilliant planner, who delighted in the practicality achieved by asymmetries within symmetry; at Eaton he succeeded in achieving a domestic character despite using his favourite heavy French Gothic, and the main block facing the formal gardens echoed Porden's earlier mansion by being symmetrical. The necessary picturesque asymmetry was, however, achieved by the 183-ft high clock tower, which rose above the large chapel placed on

▲ The grand staircase at Eaton Hall, photographed by G.B. Mason in 1959.

one side; its carillon played 'Home, Sweet Home' whenever the Duke was in residence.

The interior was, of course, solid and sumptuous: the drawing room decorated with paintings of the Canterbury Pilgrims by Stacy Marks. In the entrance hall was a floor of pietra dura; the grand staircase lined with suits of armour. Everywhere were elaborately carved pointed arches rising above marble shafts. Photographs suggest the interior of the house was not unlike that of an ambitious town hall in a proud Northern city, and in many ways Eaton Hall was an institution rather than a house. It had 150 bedrooms and needed 50 indoor servants and 40 gardeners to keep it running.

'Now that I have built a palace, I *wish* I lived in a cottage,' wrote the Duke to his daughter-in-law in 1881 when the work was complete, but he was driven by a sense of duty and thought of himself as the head of a great public institution or trust. As Mark Girouard points out, much of his income went to charity and, 'his park at Eaton Hall was always open to the public and, during his life, on the Eaton Hall estate alone, he built 48 farmhouses, 360 cottages, 8 schools, 7 village halls and 3 churches'.[147]

When he died in 1899, he was described in *The Times* as, 'a fine example of the great noble who, while following the same pursuits and amusements as other Englishmen of wealth and leisure, devotes a great part of his time to the service of those less fortunate than himself'. His successor, the 2nd Duke – the odious 'Bend Or' – cared less for duty and for Eaton Hall. The house was neglected in favour of his other seats although, in the 1930s, one of his several Duchesses made an attempt to modernise the interior.

The problem of the house seemed to be solved with the Second World War, when it was first requisitioned by the Royal Navy and was then let on a long lease to the Army as an officers' training college. But with the ending of National Service, the War Office surrendered the lease. In 1953, the 2nd Duke died and the Grosvenor Estate trustees decided that no future Duke would ever live at Eaton again. The great pile was demolished in 1961–63 – apart from the stable court and the chapel. This despite protests by the Victorian Society and the suggestion that the house, if unwanted, could be used as the nucleus of a new Chester University, as such institutions were then being founded all over the country. That was a use which surely would have appealed to the 1st Duke, but his successors claimed no use could be found for his prodigious creation.

In the event, the 5th Duke, who inherited in 1967, decided that he *did* in fact want to live at Eaton and in 1970 commissioned a modern house to be built on the cleared site from John Dennys, which was rather reminiscent of a British Embassy in, say, Lagos. This house has since been remodelled by the 6th Duke.

Around 1870 there was a reaction against such rather ponderous and serious Gothic houses in favour of something less brash and more old-fashioned, domestic and – the word of the time – 'quaint'. The pioneers were Richard Norman Shaw and his sometime partner, William Eden Nesfield, and, from the study of traditional vernacular architecture found in old country manor houses, cottages and barns, developed the style they called 'Old English', which used timber as well as brick, tile-hung walls and leaded-light windows.

Shaw's early and influential masterpiece in this manner was LEYS WOOD, built in 1868–69 around a courtyard on an elevated site near Groombridge in Sussex. The client was his cousin James Temple, by now managing director of the Shaw Savill shipping line (see page 83). Shaw's biographer, Andrew Saint, wrote,

> It was the queen of the Groombridge houses, dominant upon the very highest rocks that could be found. Approached from below up a sinuous ascending drive, it started up from the crag like a sort of citadel in a romantic burst of dull-red brickwork and tilework, dark windows and fierce oversailing chimneys.

There was something ship-like about this, and other of his houses as, 'The sea was in Shaw's veins, whether he knew it or not. More than any other great English architect, he spent a lifetime designing ships upon land'.[148] For Hermann Muthesius, the contemporary German chronicler of *Das Englishe Haus*, there was still something Gothic about Leys Wood,

The individuality of design which is manifest here in the gate-house as well as in the whole disposition of the buildings distinguishes each of Norman Shaw's works afresh. [He] is the first in the history of nineteenth-century architecture to show this freedom from the trammels of style.[149]

The bird's-eye view pen perspective drawing of Leys Wood that Shaw exhibited at the Royal Academy in 1870 caused a sensation and, as reproduced in journals, influenced domestic architecture on both sides of the Atlantic. Unfortunately, Leys Wood, like so many large houses requisitioned by the military, was badly treated in the Second World War. In the mid-1950s, the then owner therefore pulled most of it down, but spared the tall gatehouse that Muthesius admired. The disappearance of Shaw's early masterpiece is a major loss to English architecture.

Shaw's DAWPOOL at Thurstaton, on the Wirral peninsular in Cheshire, overlooking the river Dee, was considerably larger and grandly Tudor in style rather than Olde English; there was nothing 'quaint' about it. The house was built in 1882–86 for Thomas Henry Ismay, a self-made man who went into the Liverpool shipbroking business and created the prosperous White Star Line. Ismay wanted something impressive and solid; only the best would do, so no nails were used in the construction: only brass screws.

Andrew Saint writes that, 'To judge from photographs, the mood of Thomas Ismay's house was alternately fearsome and ghostly, lowing in shadow and rainfall, bleaching balefully in sunlight, in accord with the rich, but chilly red of the Wirral sandstone from which it was fashioned'.[150] *Country Life*, on the other hand, considered it in 1911 to be, 'an acknowledged masterpiece, familiar and honoured wherever English architecture is held in esteem'.[151] But it had a short life. Ismay died in 1899 and his son, Joseph Bruce Ismay – whose reputation would later be tarnished by the *Titanic* disaster – moved out of the house in 1907. 'Poor old Dawpool!', Shaw wrote when he heard of this;

▶ Dawpool, Cheshire, from the gardens in the early 20th century.

▶ The picture gallery at Dawpool.

I am sorry. Perhaps it can be turned into a sanatorium or a small pox hospital. I remember Mrs Ismay saying to me more than 10 years ago, that even then it had more than answered its purpose, for it had interested and amused Mr Ismay every day of his life for 15 years![152]

The house was sold to F.W.P. Rutter, who allowed it to become an officers' orthopaedic hospital during the Great War. It was sold again to Sir Henry Roberts, who never moved in. In 1927, the house was demolished – partly with dynamite as it was so well built. Some fittings

were rescued and reused elsewhere; one grand chimneypiece found its way to Clough Williams-Ellis' Portmeirion in Wales. A new, smaller house was built on the site, but the stables survive.

George Gilbert Scott junior was particularly unlucky in terms of his architectural legacy, for not only have his two principal churches been demolished (see pages 117–18) but his only country house has also disappeared. He rebuilt and enlarged GARBOLDISHAM MANOR, near Diss in Norfolk, for Cecil Molineux-Montgomerie in about 1868–74. Scott was early in using the 'Queen Anne' style for vicarages and villas (to the dismay of his father), but for this larger country house he chose the Jacobean style.

Built of white and red brick, the house was symmetrical with elaborate Baroque gables above the projecting wings. The interior was decorated by Morris & Co. The Molineux-Mongomeries had acquired the Norfolk estate with a West Indian fortune, but Scott's client only lived in his new house for about half a dozen years as both the agricultural depression and the collapse of West Indian sugar prices brought him near to insolvency. After the 1870s the house was continuously let and the family sold the estate in the 1930s and 1940s. Garboldisham Manor was damaged by fire and demolished – apart from the stables – in 1954. This was at the height of the post-war holocaust of country houses and the following year, Garboldisham Old Hall, a much older house, was also burned and destroyed.

Like Scott, Philip Webb would seem unfortunate in the way posterity has treated his work. Despite the critical acclaim enjoyed by this fastidious Arts and Crafts architect, both during his lifetime and since, several of his major houses have disappeared, while others – notably Clouds and Arisaig – have been mutilated. ROUNTON GRANGE, in the North Riding of Yorkshire, was built in 1873–76 for the iron-master, scientist and collector, Isaac Lothian Bell, whose family would become one of Webb's most important and sympathetic clients.

The architect was inspired by both Border pele towers and by Elizabethan houses but, as always, transformed historical precedents into something personal and modern. This house was superbly built, with ochre-coloured local sandstone used externally while the roofs were covered in (then unfashionable) red pantiles. The interior was almost entirely furnished and decorated with work by Morris & Co., much of it designed by Webb. In the panelled dining room was a frieze by Edward Burne-Jones and a ceiling decorated by Morris.

Sheila Kirk, Webb's modern biographer, found that many who remembered it described Rounton Grange as a beautiful house and observed that while,

Many of Bell's fellow industrialists in Middlesbrough built heavy neo-Gothic or French château-inspired edifices outside the town. In contrast, despite its great height, Rounton Grange, a few miles further away,

was an unostentatious but dignified building, with a strong, vigorous beauty suited to North Yorkshire, and a form and restrained inventive details that reflected the architectural heritage of the area.[153]

After the Great War, the Bell family found the house expensive to run and used nearby Mount Grace Manor for most of the year. During the Second World War, it was requisitioned and ill-used by evacuees and then by Italian prisoners of war. Unable to afford to live in it or repair it, and having failed to sell it, the family offered the house to the National Trust but could not provide an endowment. Rounton Grange was dismantled between 1951 and 1954 and all the fine work by Morris and his collaborators destroyed.

JOLDWYNDS, near Holmbury St Mary in Surrey, was one of Webb's best and most influential designs, but the tragedy of its demolition has been rather overshadowed by the sensational history of its replacement. The house was built in 1872–74 for the distinguished eye surgeon William Bowman, later made a baronet. Webb designed it in his own subtle version of 'Old English', which he developed to create a national vernacular way of building. Georgian sashed windows were combined with tile-hung walls, weather-boarded gables and tall, powerful brick chimneys.

In the 1880s and 1890s, the house was much visited and admired by younger architects, and Webb's powerful motif of triple gables would appear in houses designed by Ernest Newton and Edwin Lutyens. Webb's first biographer, the Arts and Crafts architect and writer, W.R. Lethaby, recalled in 1925 that, 'The thing itself in its place, when I saw it many years ago, was most delightful; it looked as if human people might live in it – a very difficult criterion for a modern dwelling'.[154]

Unfortunately, despite all this, within just a few years Webb's masterpiece was frivolously replaced by a building in an aesthetic inspired not by human values but by machines. Joldwynds was bought by the barrister Wilfrid Greene, later Master of the Rolls, knighted and ennobled, who demolished it in 1930 and commissioned a flashy, photogenic Modern Movement house to be built in its mature grounds by the fashionable architect Oliver Hill – who ought to have known better. However, the new Joldwynds, built in 1931–32,

proved unsatisfactory. The flat roofs leaked, the cement render fell off the walls and the client found the hard surfaces of the interior uncomfortable, the architect-designed furniture cumbersome and the house was as expensive to run as its predecessor.

Greene sued Hill for compensation, sold the house and in 1938–39 built another modernist house (but with a pitched roof) designed by Lubetkin and Tecton, higher up on the site. Such were the consequences of fashionable anti-Victorian prejudice, for surely the wretched Green would have been better off keeping Webb's house.

FONTHILL HOUSE, the last of the six country houses at Fonthill to be demolished (so far: see page 117), was also a magnificent Arts & Crafts creation – just the sort of house that has long been preferred to Victorian piles. Originally called LITTLE RIDGE, it was built in 1904–06 for Charles Morrison, whose family had been steadily acquiring most of the Fonthill Estate since James Morrison, said to be the richest commoner in England, bought Fonthill Splendens in the 1820s.

Charles Morrison's architect was Detmar Jellings Blow, a disciple of Ruskin and Morris, who has been categorised as one of the 'Wandering Architects': Arts & Crafts architects who, when young, learned about building by working with their own hands on site. But Little Ridge was not entirely a new house, for its core was the old manor house at nearby Berwick St Leonard which, in 1905, was derelict and roofless. Blow carefully took this house down and re-erected it convincingly at Fonthill by using craftsmen skilled in traditional building techniques.

Unfortunately, Little Ridge was extended by Blow in the same Elizabethan style and manner, in 1908 and again after 1912. This turned it, 'into the sort of Edwardian dinosaur whose future was uncertain as soon as the "House in the Country" superseded the "Country House" in the public imagination'.[155] However, the Morrisons could well afford to live there, and it was renamed Fonthill House in 1921, after the remains of Alderman Beckford's eponymous house were demolished.

Blow's house was inherited by Major John Granville Morrison, Conservative MP for Salisbury; created Baron Margadale in 1965. Soon afterwards, this ineffable grandee, who had already destroyed Burn's Fonthill Abbey (see above) and who was, by now, Lord-Lieutenant of Wiltshire and, indeed, president of the county's historic buildings trust, proposed to demolish his seat. Learning of this, the Victorian Society made an urgent request that it be spot-listed, but the Department of the Environment decided this was

not justified. Subsequently it emerged that this was because an inspector, after a telephone conversation with Lord Margadale, had mistakenly assumed the house had been badly damaged by fire and subsequently rebuilt when it was the other, earlier, Fonthill House that burned (in 1919). By the time the Department realised the mistake and admitted that, 'there would have been a strong case for spot-listing, and a possibility that the demolition would not have been allowed to proceed', it was too late.

What the Victorian Society considered, 'one of the most notable of early-20th century country houses' was demolished in 1972 and replaced by a Neo-Georgian house designed by Trenwith Wills. Detmar Blow's creation has the melancholy distinction of being one of the very last country houses to be deliberately demolished and, 'Future generations are sure to condemn the avoidable loss of this very fine house'.[156]

To conclude this sad survey of lost Victorian architecture, an extraordinary building at once a memorial, a country cottage and a folly. William Mackworth-Dolben was a younger son of Sir Digby Mackworth, Bt, who had taken an additional surname having married the heiress of Sir John English Dolben of Finedon in Northamptonshire, also a baronet.

Mackworth-Dolben was an enthusiastic amateur architect who not only enlarged and Gothicised his seat, Finedon Hall, but also built the Bell Inn and several houses in the village. His most remarkable creation was the VOLTA TOWER, built in 1865. This was named not directly after the eponymous Italian physicist but after a naval vessel, *HMS Volta*, on which his son, William Digby Mackworth-Dolben, a naval officer, was serving when he drowned at sea, off the African coast in 1863. (Mackworth-Dolben was unlucky: another son, the poet Digby Mackworth-Dolben, a friend of Gerard Manley Hopkins, died at the age of 19 a few years later, in 1867 – also by drowning but this time in a river in Warwickshire.)

The memorial tower combined a gabled cottage with a squat circular chimney-like erection, which terminated in machicolations and battlements. Like the follies built by Sir Thomas Tresham in the same county three centuries earlier, the Volta Tower was built of contrasting courses of Northamptonshire ironstone and a

light grey limestone. As with his other creations, in designing this strange building Mackworth-Dolben enjoyed the assistance of the Northampton architect Edmund F. Law, who must have been familiar with the tough, vigorous High Victorian creations of S.S. Teulon while the ring of stubby columns around the tower recalls the work of 'Greek' Thomson of Glasgow.

The architectural amateurism of the Squire of Finedon may have been responsible for the ultimate downfall of his tower, for it suddenly collapsed in November 1951 – killing the wife of its then tenant – and it was afterwards discovered that, surprisingly, no mortar had been used in its construction. It is rare to discover a Victorian building that perished through faulty construction rather than malevolent intent.

REFERENCES

INTRODUCTION

1 P.G. Wodehouse, *Summer Moonshine*, London, n.d. [1938], pp. 22–23.
2 James Laver, *Victoriana*, London and Melbourne, 1966, p. 9.
3 Kenneth Clark, *The Gothic Revival: An Essay in the History of Taste*, 2nd edn, London, 1949, p. 2.
4 *The Victorian Society Annual Report 1967-8*, p. 4.
5 Foreword to Alison and Peter Smithson, *The Euston Arch and the Growth of the London, Midland & Scottish Railway*, London, 1968.
6 John Betjeman, 'Introduction' in Peter Ferriday (ed), *Victorian Architecture*, London, 1963, p. 15.
7 H.S. Goodhart-Rendel, 'Victorian Conservanda' in *The Journal of the London Society*, November 1958, p. 47.
8 Virginia Woolf, *Orlando: A Biography*, London, 1928, p. 222.
9 Robert Byron, 'New Delhi', *The Architectural Review*, January 1931, p. 1.
10 G.M. Trevelyan, *English Social History*, London, 1944, p. 524.
11 *Ideas and Beliefs of the Victorians*, London, 1949, p. 15.
12 Nikolaus Pevsner, 'Victorian Prolegomena' in Ferriday, 1963, *op. cit.*, p. 12.
13 'Victorian Conservanda', *op. cit.*, p. 39.
14 Kenneth Clark, *The Gothic Revival: An Essay in the History of Taste*, London, 1928, p. vii.
15 Clark, 1949, p. 2.
16 Basil F.L. Clarke, *Church Builders of the Nineteenth Century*, 2nd edn, Newton Abbot, 1969, p. vi.
17 Sir Reginald Blomfield, *Richard Norman Shaw, R.A.: Architect 1831-1912*, London, 1940, p. v.
18 Evelyn Waugh, *A Handful of Dust*, London, 1934, p. 29.
19 John Summerson, 'The Evaluation of Victorian Architecture' in the *Victorian Society Annual 1968-9*, pp. 45–46, and in *Victorian Architecture: Four Studies in Evaluation*, New York and London, 1970, p. 16.
20 John Summerson, 'Act 3: Christian Gothic. Scene 1: William Butterfield' in the *Architectural Review* xcviii, December 1945, pp. 170 and 172.
21 John Summerson, *Heavenly Mansions*, London, 1949, p. 198.
22 quoted in Frank Kelsall, 'Not As Ugly as Stonehenge: Architecture and History in the First Lists of Historic Buildings', *Architectural History* 52 (2009), p. 17.
23 Stephen Games (ed), *Pevsner on Art and Architecture: The Radio Talks*, London, 2002, p. 87.
24 Ralph Dutton, *The Victorian Home*, London, 1954, p. 82.
25 Reginald Turnor, *Nineteenth Century Architecture in Britain*, London, 1950, pp. 68 and 91.
26 *The Times*, 4 February 1956, p. 7.
27 Mark Girouard, 'The Evolving Taste for Victorian Architecture' in *Apollo*, February 1973, p. 129.
28 *Daily Express*, 5 October 1967, and in James Knox, *Cartoons & Coronets: the Genius of Osbert Lancaster*, London, 2008, p. 215.
29 quoted in Gavin Stamp, *Alexander 'Greek' Thomson*, London, 1999, pp. 24–25.
30 Pevsner to Glasgow City Planning Office, 17 February 1966; *Glasgow Herald*, 4 March 1966.
31 *The Victorian Society Annual Report 1959-60*, pp. 4–5.
32 n.d.; copy in Victorian Society archives.
33 see Gavin Stamp, 'Origins of the [Georgian] Group' in the *Architects' Journal*, clxxv, 31 March 1982 and Gavin Stamp, 'Early Twentieth-Century Stations' in Julian Holder and Steven Parissien (eds), *The Architecture of British Transport in the Twentieth Century*, New Haven and London, 2004.

34 see in particular Alison and Peter Smithson, *The Euston Arch and the Growth of the London, Midland & Scottish Railway*, London, 1968. The leader was apparently written by the editor himself, Sir William Haley.
35 *The Victorian Society Report 1961-1962*, p. 3.
36 J.M. Richards, *Memoirs of an Unjust Fella*, London, 1980, p. 127.
37 *The Times*, 6 June 1961, p. 13.
38 *The Victorian Society Report 1962-1963*, p. 5.
39 *The Victorian Society Report 1963-1964*, p. 8.
40 *The Victorian Society Annual Report 1966*, p. 16.
41 *Foreign & Commonwealth Office*, HMSO, London, 1991.
42 *The Victorian Society Annual 1972-73*, p. 8.
43 for the threats to both Euston and St Pancras in the 1930s, see Stamp (2004), *op. cit.*, pp. 40–43.
44 *The Victorian Society Annual Report 1966*, p. 8.
45 John Betjeman, 'Temple to the Age of Steam' in the *Weekend Telegraph*, 11 November 1966, p. 48. *St Pancras Station* by Jack Simmons was published in 1968.
46 Candida Lycett-Green (ed), *John Betjeman Letters, volume two, 1951 to 1984*, London, 1995, p. 319.
47 Sir John Summerson, 'Red Elephant in the Euston Road' in the *Illustrated London News*, ccli, October 1967, p. 18.
48 for Betjeman's work with the Victorian Society, see Gavin Stamp, 'A Lightweight Wax Fruit Merchant?, or, John Betjeman and Conservation' in *First and Last Loves: John Betjeman & Architecture*, Sir John Soane's Museum, London, 2006.
49 *The Victorian Society Annual 1976*, p. 5, quoting Vivian Lipman.
50 see Gavin Stamp, 'I was Lord Kitchener's Valet or, How the Vic Soc Saved London' in Elain Harwood and Alan Powers (eds), *Twentieth Century Architecture 6. The Sixties: life : style : architecture*, London, 2002, pp. 129–44.
51 Ian Nairn, *Britain's Changing Towns*, London, 1967, pp. 7, 63 and 64.
52 Ian Nairn, *Nairn's London*, Harmondsworth, 1966, p. 186.
53 John Betjeman, 'A preservationist's progress' in Jane Fawcett (ed), *The Future of the Past: Attitudes to Conservation 1174-1974*, London, 1976, p. 55.
54 Robert Furneaux Architecture, *Victorian Architecture*, Harmondsworth, 1966, p. 18.
55 Goodhart-Rendel (1958), *op. cit.*, p. 39.

1 IRON AND GLASS

1 Raymond McGrath and A.C. Frost, *Glass in Architecture and Decoration*, London, 1937, p. 125.
2 *Daily Express*, 2 December 1936.
3 Violet R. Markham, *Paxton and the Batchelor Duke*, London, 1935, p. 121.
4 McGrath and Frost, 1937, p. 211.
5 Christopher Hammond, *The Good, the Bad and the Ugly: An Architectural Walk Through Bradford City Centre and Little Germany*, Bradford, 2006, p. 10.
6 Simon H. Adamson, *Seaside Piers*, London, 1977, p.108.

2 RAILWAYS

7 Quoted in Jeffrey Richards and John M. MacKenzie, *The Railway Station: A Social History*, Oxford, 1986, p. 20.
8 David Pearce and Marcus Binney (eds), *Off The Rails: Saving Railway Architecture*, London, 1977, p. 4.
9 Marcus Binney and David Pearce (eds), *Railway Architecture*, London, 1979, p. 12.
10 *The Times*, 11 June 1960.
11 Foreword to Alison and Peter Smithson, *The Euston Arch and*

the *Growth of the London, Midland & Scottish Railway*, London, 1968.

12 John Betjeman, 'London Railway Stations' in *First and Last Loves*, London, 1952, p. 80.

13 *Architectural Review*, April 1962, p. 238.

14 Christian Barman, *An Introduction to Railway Architecture*, London, 1950, p. 84.

15 *The Builder*, 2 October 1942, p. 282.

16 John Betjeman, *London's Historic Railway Stations*, London, 1972, p. 50.

17 C. Hamilton Ellis, *British Trains of Yesteryear*, London, 1960.

18 John Betjeman, 'London Railway Stations' in *First and Last Loves*, London, 1952, p. 87.

19 Quoted in John Thomas, *A Regional History of the Railways of Great Britain* (vol.vi), *Scotland: The Lowlands and The Borders*, Newton Abbot, 1984, p. 231.

20 *Builder*, 9 July 1898, quoted in Colin Johnston and John R. Hume, *Glasgow Stations*, Newton Abbot, 1979, p. 116.

3 HOTELS AND BUILDINGS FOR PLEASURE

21 Betjeman, 1972, p. 66.

22 Nikolaus Pevsner, *The Buildings of England: London Except the Cities of London & Westminster*, Harmondsworth, 1952, p. 217.

23 Quoted in Hermione Hobhouse, *Lost London*, London, 1971, p. 207.

24 Hobhouse, 1971, *op. cit.*, p. 211.

25 *Dickens's Dictionary of London, 1888*, p. 215.

26 John Earl, *British Theatres and Music Halls*, Princes Risborough, 2005, pp. 45-46.

27 John Earl, 'The London Theatres' in Brian Mercer Walker (ed), *Frank Matcham: Theatre Architect*, Belfast, 1980, pp. 43-44.

28 Godfrey James, *London: The Western Reaches*, London, 1950, p. 280.

29 Earl, 1980, p. 40.

30 Nikolaus Pevsner, *The Buildings of England: London I, the Cities of London & Westminster*, Harmondsworth, 1957, p. 296.

31 Mark Girouard, *Victorian Pubs*, London, 1975, p. 10.

32 *Time Gentlemen, Please!*, London, 1983, p. 3.

33 Alan Crawford, Michael Dunn and Robert Thorne, *Birmingham Pubs 1880-1939*, Gloucester, 1986, p. 21.

34 Pevsner, *The Buildings of England: South Lancashire*, Harmondsworth, 1969, p. 175.

4 COMMERCE

35 Henry-Russell Hitchcock, *Early Victorian Architecture*, vol.i, London & New Haven, 1954, p. 316.

36 David Watkin, *The Life and Work of C.R. Cockerell*, London, 1974, p. 227.

37 H.S. Goodhart-Rendel, 'Victorian Conservanda' in *The Journal of the London Society*, November 1958, p. 41.

38 Sir John Summerson, *The Victorian Rebuilding of the City of London*, Cornell, 1974, p. 10; Pevsner, *London I*, 1957, p. 248.

39 Pevsner, *London I*, 1957, p. 224; Simon Bradsley and Nikolaus Pevsner, *The Buildings of England: London I, The City of London*, London, 1997, p. 536.

40 *The Victorian Society Annual Report, 1955-1966*, p. 21.

41 *The Victorian Society Report, 1963-1964*, p. 10.

42 Henry-Russell Hitchcock, 'Early Cast Iron Façades' in *The Architectural Review*, February 1951, p. 114.

43 Letter to Pevsner 1949, quoted in Gavin Stamp, *Alexander 'Greek' Thomson*, London, 1999, p. 169.

44 Hammond, 2006, *op.cit.*, p. 22.

45 Derek Lindstrum, *West Yorkshire: Architects and Architecture*, London, 1978, p. 298.

46 Henry-Russell Hitchcock, *Architecture: Nineteenth and Twentieth Centuries*, Harmondsworth, 1963, p. 237: the other was the extant Gothic warehouse in Stokes Croft, Bristol, by E.W. Godwin.

47 Nikolaus Pevsner, *The Buildings of England. Yorkshire: The West Riding*, Harmondsworth, 1959, p. 317.

48 Edward Walford, *Old and New London*, vol. v, London n.d. (c. 1879-85), p. 506.

49 Pevsner, *London*, 1952, p. 70.

50 Goodhart-Rendel, 1958, p. 40.

51 Marcus Binney, *SAVE Britain's Heritage 1975-2005: Thirty Years of Campaigning*, London, 2005, p. 226.

52 Quoted in Summerson, *The Victorian Rebuilding of the City of London*, Cornell, 1974, p. 29.

53 Sir John Summerson, *The Architecture of Victorian London*, Charlottesville, 1976, p. 54, and Summerson, 1974, p. 30.

54 Quoted in Hobhouse, 1971, p. 168.

55 Andor Gomme and David Walker, *Architecture of Glasgow*, London, 1968, pp. 205-09.

5 INDUSTRIAL

56 Kenneth Powell, 'New Uses' in Marcus Binney, Ron Fitzgerald, Randolph Langenbach and Ken Powell, *Satanic Mills* (London n.d. [1979]), pp. 42-43.

57 Randolph Langenbach, 'The Challenge Facing Oldham' in *Satanic Mills*, 1979, pp. 16-18.

6 PLACES OF WORSHIP

58 Ken Powell, *The Fall of Zion: Northern Chapel Architecture and Its Future*, SAVE Britain's Heritage, 1980.

59 Quoted in Andrew Saint, *Richard Norman Shaw*, New Haven & London, 1976, p. 61.

60 Saint, 1976, p. 63.

61 Quoted in Pevsner, *London*, 1957, p. 437.

62 A. Welby Pugin, *The Present State of Ecclesiastical Architecture in England*, London, 1843, p. 102.

63 Nikolaus Pevsner, *The Buildings of England: Yorkshire The West Riding*, Harmondsworth, 1959, p. 71.

64 Rosemary Hill, *God's Architect: Pugin & the Building of Romantic Britain*, London, 2007, p. 270.

65 Frank Worsdall, *The City that Disappeared: Glasgow's Demolished Architecture*, Glasgow, 1981, p. 87.

66 Worsdall, 1981, p. 85.

67 Scott, p. 88.

68 Quoted in Paul Thompson, *William Butterfield*, London, 1971, p. 239.

69 Hitchcock, 1954, p. 595.

70 Nikolaus Pevsner, *The Buildings of England: North Somerset and Bristol*, Harmondsworth, 1958, p. 387.

71 Andor Gomme, Michael Jenner and Bryan Little, *Bristol: An architectural History*: London, 1979, p. 307.

72 John Summerson, 'The Past in the Future' in *Heavenly Mansions*, London, 1949, p. 238.

73 Pevsner, *London*, 1952, p. 362; Paul Thompson (ed), *The High Victorian Cultural Achievement*, The Victorian Society, 1967.

74 H.S. Goodhart-Rendel, 'Rogue Architects of the Victorian Era', *RIBA Journal*, April 1949, p. 251.

75 James Stevens Curl, *Victorian Architecture: Its Practical Aspects*, Newton Abbot, 1973, p. 53.

76 *The Victorian Society Annual, 1972-73*, p. 19.

77 Basil F.L. Clarke, *Parish Churches of London*, London, 1966, p. 147; Goodhart-Rendel, 1949, *op. cit.*, p. 255.

78 *Glasgow Evening Times* 1893, quoted in Gavin Stamp, *Alexander 'Greek' Thomson*, London, 1999, p. 174.

79 Clyde Binfield, *The Contexting of a Chapel Architect: James Cubitt 1836-1912*, London, 2001, p. 71.

80 Sharman Kadish (ed), *Building Jerusalem: Jewish Architecture in Britain*, London, 1996, pp. 2, 6 and 12.

81 Carol Herselle Krinsky in Kadish, *op. cit.*, p. 27.

82 *Victorian Society Annual 1985-86*, p. 33.

83 J.M. Richards (ed), *The Bombed Buildings of Britain*, London, 1942, p. 49.

84 *Bombed Churches as war memorials*, London, 1945, p.7; Pevsner, *London*, 1952, p. 207.

85 T.F. Bumpus, *London Churches, Ancient and Modern* (London, n.d. [*c.* 1907]), p. 356.

86 Quoted in Gavin Stamp, *An Architect of Promise: George Gilbert Scott Junior (1839-1897) and the Late Gothic Revival* (Donington, 2002), p. 90.

87 Bumpus, *op. cit.*, p. 359.

88 Saint, *op. cit.*, p. 274.

89 John Hadfield [ed], *The Saturday Book 19*, London, 1959, p. 68

90 P.G. Rogers, *The Sixth Trumpeter: The Story of Jezreel and his Tower*, London, 1963, p. 135.

7 PUBLIC BUILDINGS

91 Derek Linstrum, *Towers and Colonnades: The Architecture of Cuthbert Brodrick*, Leeds, 1999, p. 109.

92 Linstrum, *op. cit.*, p. 75.

93 *Victorian Society Annual 1981*, p. 22; Bridget Cherry and Nikolaus Pevsner, *The Buildings of England: London 3 North West*, London, 1991, p. 427.

94 H.S. Goodhart-Rendel, *English Architecture Since the Regency*, London, 1953, p. 172.

95 *The Times*, 10 February 1956, 13 February 1956, 24 February 1956.

96 Asa Briggs, *Victorian Cities*, London, 1963, p. 217.

97 Ian Nairn, *Britain's Changing Towns*, London, 1967, p. 9.

98 Nikolaus Pevsner and Alexandra Wedgwood, *The Buildings of England: Warwickshire*, Harmondsworth, 1966, p. 119.

99 Charles L. Eastlake, *A History of the Gothic Revival*, London, 1872, p. 313.

100 A.E. Richardson, *Monumental Classic Architecture in Great Britain and Ireland During the Eighteenth & Nineteenth Centuries*, London, 1914, p. 108.

8 PUBLIC AND PRIVATE INSTITUTIONS

101 Briggs, 1963, p. 24.

102 Joe Holyoak in *The Victorian*, March 2007, p. 7.

103 Ian Gordon and Simon Inglis, *Great Lengths: The Historic Indoor Swimming Pools of Britain*, Swindon, 2009, pp. 13 and 17.

104 *Taking the Plunge: The Architecture of Bathing*, SAVE Britain's Heritage, n.d.[1982]), pp. 16–18.

105 Sarah Rutherford, *The Victorian Asylum*, Oxford, 2008, pp.1–2.

106 *Mind Over Matter: A Study of the Country's Threatened Mental Asylums*, SAVE Britain's Heritage 1995, pp. 1 and 8.

107 Quoted in J. Mordaunt Crook, 'Sydney Smirke' in Jane Fawcett [ed], *Seven Victorian Architects*, London, 1976, p. 60.

108 Briggs, 1963, p. 44.

109 *New Statesman*, 16 October 2000.

110 Quoted in David Walker, 'Sir John James Burnet' in Alastair Service [ed], *Edwardian Architecture and Its Origins*, London, 1975, p. 193.

111 Quoted in Girouard, 1977, *op. cit.*, p. 56.

112 'The Naval Treaty', 1893, quoted in Girouard, 1977, *op. cit.*, p. 64.

113 Pevsner, *South Lancashire, op. cit.*, 1969, p. 48; 'Nine Swallows – No Summer', 1942, in Nikolaus Pevsner and J.M. Richards [eds], *The Anti-Rationalists*, London, 1973, pp. 207–08.

114 Philip H. Goare, *Spike Island: The Memory of a Military Hospital*, London, 2001, pp. 1–2.

115 N. Pevsner and D. Lloyd, *The Buildings of England: Hampshire and the Isle of Wight*, Harmondsworth, 1967, p. 350.

116 *Mind over Matter, op. cit.*, p. 3.

117 Pevsner, *South Lancashire*, 1969, p. 169; Quentin Hughes, *Seaport: Architecture & Townscape in Liverpool*, London, 1964, p. 48.

118 Goodhart-Rendel, 1958, *op. cit.*, p. 43.

9 DOMESTIC ARCHITECTURE. URBAN AND SUBURBAN

119 E. Beresford Chancellor, *The Private Palaces of London, Past and Present*, London, 1908, p. 250.

120 *The Times*, 16 July 1929.

121 David Pearce, *London's Mansions: The Palatial Houses of the Nobility*, London, 1986, p. 130.

122 Mark Girouard, *Sweetness and Light: The 'Queen Anne' Movement 1860-1900*, London, 1977, pp. 38–39.

123 Mrs. Haweis, *Beautiful Houses; Being a Description of Certain Well-Known Artistic Houses*, 3rd edition, London, 1889, p. 91.

124 *The Victorian Society Annual, 1969-70*, pp. 11–12.

125 T. Affleck Greeves, *Guide to Bedford Park in the Form of Two Walks*, London, 1983, p. 15.

126 *The Annual Report of the Chelsea Society 1962*, pp. 31–32.

127 Quoted in Susan Weber Soros [ed], *E.W. Godwin: Aesthetic Movement Architect and Designer*, New Haven & London, 1999, p. 168.

128 *ex info.* Susie Harries; Alan Crawford, *C.R. Ashbee: Architect, Designer & Romantic Socialist*, New Haven & London, 1985, p. 259.

129 Crawford, *op. cit.*, p. 259.

130 Francis Worsdall, *The Tenement: A Way of Life*, Edinburgh, 1979, p. 59.

131 Worsdall, 1981, p. 72.

132 Rosemary Hill, *God's Architect: Pugin & the Building of Romantic Britain*, London, 2007, p. 233.

133 Pevsner, *South Lancashire*, 1969, p. 210.

134 *The Victorian Society Annual, 1969-70*, p. 14.

135 *The Victorian Society Annual Report, 1965–66*, p. 10.

136 Quoted in Richard Wildman, 'The Houses of Usher' in *Architectural Association Quarterly*, January 1970, p. 70.

137 Hugh Casson, *An Introduction to Victorian Architecture*, London, 1948, p. 84; Joan Evans, *The Victorians*, Cambridge, 1966, plate 72.

138 Nikolaus Pevsner, *Buildings of England: Hertfordshire*, Harmondsworth, 1953, p. 77.

10 COUNTRY HOUSES

139 Mark Girouard, *The Victorian Country House*, Oxford, 1971, p.vii.

140 Michael Hall, *The Victorian Country House*, London, 2009, p. 7.

141 John Summerson, 'Our Heritage in Architecture', *Picture Post*, 3 January 1942, p. 24.

142 *The Victorian Society Annual Report, 1966*, p. 30.

143 Girouard, 1971, *op. cit.*, p. 59.

144 David Walker, 'William Burn' in Jane Fawcett [ed], *Seven Victorian Architects*, London, 1976, p. 31.

145 Osbert Lancaster, *Pillar to Post*, London, 1938, p. 50.

146 Valerie Fiddes and Alistair Rowan, *David Bryce 1803-1876*, Edinburgh, 1976, p. 9.

147 Girouard, 1971, *op. cit.*, p. 1.

148 Saint, 1976, *op. cit.*, p. 43.

149 Hermann Muthesius, *The English House*, London, 2007, vol.i, pp. 115 and 117.

150 Saint, 1976, *op. cit.*, p. 261.

151 Quoted in Giles Worsley, *England's Lost Houses*, London, 2002, p. 56.

152 Quoted in Saint, 1976, *op. cit.*, p. 263.

153 Sheila Kirk, *Philip Webb: Pioneer of Arts & Crafts Architecture*, Chichester, 2005, p. 125.

154 W.R. Lethaby, *Philip Webb and His Work*, Oxford, 1935, p. 92.

155 Michael Drury, *Wandering Architects: In Pursuit of an Arts and Crafts Ideal*, Stamford, 2000, p. 130.

156 *The Victorian Society Annual, 1971-72*, p. 38; *The Times*, 12 June 1972, p. 12.

ACKNOWLEDGEMENTS

I am particularly grateful to Colin Cunningham, past chairman, and Ian Dungavell, director of the Victorian Society, for initially asking me to assemble material for an exhibition to celebrate the 50th birthday of the society in 2008, from which, thanks to Graham Coster at the Aurum Press, this present book emerged. A majority of the photographs of demolished Victorian buildings here reproduced come from the National Monuments Record, now administered by English Heritage, whose staff at Swindon were unfailingly helpful – above all Ian Leith, who knows more about historic photographs than anyone alive. For help in locating or providing other photographs and for other information, I am most grateful to the following: John H.G. Archer, David Beevers, Oliver Bradbury, Ken Brand, Mosette Broderick, Robert Carr, Martin Charles, Alan Crawford, Michael Hall, Susie Harries, Rosemary Hill, Sheila Kirk, Harry Jack, Simon P. Johnson, Randolph Langenbach, John Minnis, the Revd Christopher Pearson, Jan Piggott, Kenneth Powell, Aileen Reid, Lisa Rigg, Elizabeth Robinson, Andrew Saint, Jamie Smith, Robert Thorne, Andrew Vine, David M. Walker, Mark Watson and Richard Wildman as well as Will Palin and Robert Hradsky at SAVE Britain's Heritage and any others I fear I may have forgotten. As for a bibliography for what is, in essence, both a history and historiography of Victorian architecture illustrated with demolished examples, the many books consulted for the text will be found in the References.

PICTURE CREDITS

Country Life: front endpapers, 33, 49 (top), 157 (bottom), 163 (bottom right), 175 (top), 176, 177, 184, 186
Royal Institute of British Architects: 2-3, 64, 79, 121, 183
Glasgow Museums: 6, 109
English Heritage/National Monuments Record: 8-9, 16 (top), 17 (top), 20, 21, 25, 34, 35, 37, 45 (top right, bottom), 46, 48, 54 (top), 58, 60, 65, 66, 69, 73 (top), 76, 78 (bottom), 79 (top), 83, 84, 85, 94, 96, 97, 98, 99, 103 (top), 104, 105, 106, 107, 108, 112 (top), 113, 114, 115, 116, 118 (top), 119 (bottom), 127, 128. 129, 131, 134, 138, 140, 142, 151, 152, 154, 156, 157 (top), 158, 159, 163 (bottom left), 164, 165 (top), 166, 169 (top), 170, 172, 175 (bottom), 179, 182, rear endpapers
Estate of Osbert Lancaster: 13, 18 (bottom)
Piet Pulford: 15
Ronald Searle: 16 (bottom)
Lancashire County Library & Information Services: 17 (bottom), 125
Manchester Libraries: 18 (top), 130, 132
Royal Commission for the Ancient & Historical Monuments of Scotland: 19, 53, 56, 74, 86, 100 (bottom), 101 (bottom), 102, 163 (top), 178
PA Photos: 26
Royal Commission on the Ancient and Historical Monuments of Wales: 28, 112 (bottom)
Author's collection: 30, 55, 77, 82 (top), 91, 93, 120, 122, 167, 169 (bottom)
London Metropolitan Archives: 32, 42, 49 (bottom), 62, 73 (bottom), 80, 81, 82 (bottom), 92 (top), 111 (bottom), 144 (top), 146 (bottom), 155, 165 (bottom)
John Maltby Ltd: 38, 44
Harry Jack: 41
Mitchell Library, Glasgow City Council: 45 (top left), 75, 111 (top)
Keasbury-Gordon Photograph Archive: 47
Sir Benjamin Stone Collection, City of Birmingham Libraries: 50 (bottom)
Lens of Sutton: 51, 57

Pamlin Prints: 52 (top left)
Nick Catford: 52 (top right)
Bradford Telegraph & Argus: 52 (bottom)
Photopolis (Dundee City Council): 54 (bottom)
Ken Brand: 61
Peter Charlton: 63
John Whybrow Ltd: 67, 68
Planet News Ltd: 70
The Victorian Society: 72, 143
Yorkshire Post: 77 (bottom), 78 (top)
Randolph Langenbach: 88
Robert Carr: 90, Downside Abbey: 100 (top)
David Walker: 101 (top)
Leeds Library & Information Services: 103 (bottom)
Mosette Broderick: 110
Michael Pink: 117
Folkestone Heritage Collection © Kent County Council: 118 (bottom), 119 (top)
Francis Frith Collection: 124, 126, 150
Architectural Association: 141 (top)
T.R. Annan and Sons Ltd: 141 (bottom)
Mark Watson: 144 (middle)
Ken Roberts: 144 (bottom)
Cambridgeshire Collection: 145 (top)
John H.G. Archer: 145 (bottom)
SAVE Britain's Heritage: 146 (top)
Royal Pavilion & Museums, Brighton & Hove: 147, 148
Tacina Rae-Smith: 149
Royal Borough of Kensington & Chelsea Libraries & Arts Service: 160
Alan Crawford: 161
Judith Temple & Oliver Bradbury: 168
Harvard University, Graduate School of Design: 180
Helen Brandon-Jones: 185
Jamie Smith: 187

INDEX

Page numbers in italic refer to illustrations